healthy baking

jordan bourke

healthy baking

nourishing breads, wholesome cakes,
ancient grains and bubbling ferments

jordan bourke

contents

introduction	06
a few notes on ingredients	10
sourdough and yeasted bread	12
sweet baking	70
savoury baking	112
make a meal with it	140
ancient grains	164
preserves, dressings, and oils	198
ferments and pickles	230
index	264
acknowledgements	270

introduction

a healthy approach

I was nervous about using the word 'healthy' in the title for this book, as there has been somewhat of a backlash against the 'clean eating' movement of late. In the end, I decided to keep it in, as I believe food is there to be celebrated, not feared. I want to reclaim the word for what I believe it really means – a healthy approach to food, cooking from scratch, and a return to forgotten skills like bread making and fermentation.

The recipes in this book contain plenty of fats in things like avocados, chorizo, and olive and coconut oils. Sugars are there too, whether maple syrup, honey or coconut palm sugar. The book is also full of dishes made with complex carbohydrates from the various grains I use – rye, spelt, quinoa, brown rice, lentils and so on – most of which are also a good source of protein. Vitamins and minerals are also abundant in the great variety of fruits and vegetables I cook with, not to mention the ferments, which contain a thousand times more lactobacillus, the healthy gut bacteria, than natural yoghurt. The point is, when our grandparents harped on about 'everything in moderation' they had it absolutely right. Proteins, fats, carbohydrates, vitamins, minerals and water are the six essential nutrients needed for our bodies to survive. We need to stop victimising ingredients and find a healthy balance.

Anchoring the recipes in this book is the use of natural and whole ingredients – by which I mean they have come from the land, sea or animal with as little interference as possible, with no additives, flavourings or preservatives. That's not to say I'm obsessive though – I don't mill my own flour or boil down the sap of a coconut blossom to make my own coconut palm sugar! I'm quite happy using some ingredients that have gone through minimal processing to make them fit for purpose in a home kitchen – but I know where to draw the line. The easiest way to do this is to ask yourself whether you could, with the right equipment, make this ingredient at home if you had the time, knowledge and inclination. If the answer is yes, you should be good to go.

Of course everyone responds to ingredients in different ways, so feel free to make these recipes your own. Personally I avoid using white cane sugar, opting for coconut palm sugar instead, as I prefer its flavour. And while I enjoy some cheese now and then, I don't feel fantastic when I eat a lot of milk or cream, so I use rice, almond or coconut milk instead – but by all means use the regular version if you feel good eating it. Simply use the alternative in the recipe in the same quantities.

bread and sourdough

My love of bread, in particular the satisfying acidity of sourdough, was to a great extent born of my passion for kimchi – the ubiquitous Korean fermented vegetable dish. When I started exploring fermentation in greater detail years ago, I read more and more about its use in other kinds of ingredients, and sourdough bread was one of them. I began experimenting and was immediately hooked. The tactile pleasure of making the bread, together with how much better I feel eating it – and the knowledge of the simple goodness that goes into it – is immeasurably satisfying. Here I have included not just sourdough recipes, but also yeasted loaves, flatbreads and wraps, for the days when you don't have the time to make a sourdough from scratch. There is also a chapter full of recipes for using up any leftover bread, like the kimchi, egg, avocado and feta on sourdough, page 144, and the Italian panzanella salad, page 158. While I'm passionate about sourdough and making 'real' bread, I am by no means a 'master baker', and the chapter in this book is only the tip of the sourdough iceberg. For further reading and in-depth knowledge of the intricacies and science behind bread making, check out books like *Tartine Bread* by Chad Robertson.

fermentation and preservation

Without doubt, one of my most fulfilling and useful kitchen pursuits is fermentation and preservation. These beautiful and healthy jars of fermented, pickled and stewed fruit and vegetables fill my fridge and counter-top and have the ability to transform dishes at the last moment, with deep and exciting flavours and textures. Ferments are one of my favourite ingredients to pair with sourdough bread (a ferment in its own right), savoury bakes and grain salads, so I have included them in this book to encourage you to make them yourself at home. My wife Jina was fortunate enough to grow up in South Korea, where this kind of kitchen pastime is second nature, and that is really how it should be. In our book *Our Korean Kitchen* we covered most of the classic ferments of the country, but here I wanted to open up fermentation and pickling to a more Western audience, as it is still an area that is approached with caution by most people. In fact, it is a straightforward process and the hands-on time required is minimal, but their effect is great and they last for months. The fact that they create some of the healthiest foodstuffs in the world is just an added bonus.

grains and flours

'Ancient grains', so called as they have remained largely unchanged for thousands of years since they were first cultivated and eaten by ancient civilisations, are some of the best examples of whole natural ingredients. Spelt, quinoa, rye, buckwheat, farro, polenta, oats, barley and countless others are not just delicious to eat but are nutritionally rich and a great source of fibre, healthy fats, proteins, vitamins and minerals. I adore cooking with them, but not in a bland, vast-pots-of-boiling-lentils kind of way. They are the backbone of many sweet and savoury recipes – seasoned well and used in the right proportion with other ingredients they can be magnificent, adding texture and great flavour to everything from bread to hearty salads.

While cooking with grains could not be described as baking, I included them in this book as, when they are ground down, many of them transform into the versatile flours that I use when baking, and there is something very satisfying about using an ingredient in all its guises. Apart from that, wholegrains are delicious in so many recipes, which was reason enough to include them. My favourite all-purpose flour, both for its slightly nutty flavour and also its cooking qualities, is spelt, a cousin of wheat. However I also use smaller amounts of flours like rye, buckwheat and teff, to add a richness and depth of flavour that works so well in baked goods. I also provide optional alternatives to these more unusual flours, in case you don't have one to hand – as in most cases a straight swap for regular flour will also work.

a few notes on ingredients

Below are some key points on ingredients that are often surrounded by confusion and misinformation.

spelt flour

I use a variety of flours in my baking, but white or wholegrain spelt flour is my favourite for day-to-day use, both for its slightly nutty flavour and its similarity to wheat flour, which make it easy to cook with. However, spelt should not be considered the same as wheat. While they are related, they are two different species: spelt is Triticum spelta and wheat is Triticum aestivum. Spelt contains a lower quantity of gluten in comparison to wheat and, although unsuitable for coeliacs, those with a mild intolerance may find they have no problem tolerating spelt.

wheat is not the devil

The clean eating brigade would have you believe that wheat flour and gluten are the devil. I disagree. I believe the increasing number of people who declare themselves to have an allergy or intolerance has more to do with their consumption of commercial breads, cereals and ready meals – and the methods used to make these products – than the wheat itself. White sliced bread is a perfect example. A number of people I have cooked for over the years were convinced they had a wheat or gluten intolerance based on their body's negative reaction to the bread they had been eating, which in all cases was commercial sliced bread available in supermarkets. When they stopped eating these industrial loaves and instead ate freshly baked bread from a bakery, or started baking their own bread, with nothing more than flour, water, yeast and salt, they felt absolutely fine and all their symptoms went away. It seemed that what they had been reacting badly to was the preservatives and chemicals added to these commercial breads to achieve consistent baking performance, and not the wheat flour itself. This was a revelation to some of them, who had for years denied themselves good-quality bread and sourdough loaves. The moral of the story is that unless you are coeliac or suffer from a serious intolerance, don't be tempted to self-diagnose too quickly or cut out food groups or ingredients without seeking professional medical advice. At the time of going to print, Coeliac UK screening studies suggest that only 1 in 100 people in the UK has coeliac disease – so the chances of you being coeliac are actually quite low. Of course there are people out there with legitimate intolerances and allergies, so for those people you could try my gluten-free sandwich loaf (see page 58).

sugars and sweeteners

I love the deep caramel flavour of coconut palm sugar and use this, together with maple syrup, dried fruit and honey, instead of cane sugar in all my cooking – but feel free to use regular sugar if you prefer. Whichever sugar you use, they are all assimilated in the body in the same way so should still be eaten in moderation. We often hear that alternative sweeteners like coconut palm sugar are less refined and contain trace minerals and vitamins not present in cane sugar, and while this may be true in some cases, you would need to consume vast quantities of the sugar in question for there to be any real benefit to your health, which would defeat the purpose entirely. The good news is, wherever there is sugar in nature – i.e. fresh or dried fruit – there is also fibre. This slows down the rate at which sugar is absorbed into our blood, so you don't get the blood sugar peaks that you would with sugar on its own – for example, a spoon added into your morning tea or coffee.

extra virgin coconut oil

Coconut oil is not the miracle food that some would have you believe, but it does have a number of health benefits and is delicious, so it's worth having in your store cupboard. If you are avoiding butter, coconut oil can be used in its place in most baking recipes. In fact I know plenty of people who are not avoiding butter but still use coconut oil, as they enjoy its subtle flavour. It has a lower melting point than butter and will sometimes turn to liquid at room temperature at anything above 20°C. In savoury cooking coconut oil is also delicious, and it has a high smoking point, making it a good choice for frying. In its raw state coconut oil is known for its anti-microbial and anti-viral properties. It also contains lauric acid, a medium-chain fatty acid, which boosts immunity and supports healthy brain function. When buying coconut oil, look for brands that are described as 'extra virgin' and/or 'raw', as they will be less refined and will not have been through any heat treatment.

sourdough and yeasted bread

Real bread is made with nothing more than flour, water, yeast and salt. It is nourishing and sustaining and good for the soul. This chapter is made up of sourdoughs, yeasted loaves and quick breads, pittas, wraps and oatcakes. There is something in here to suit any occasion and any amount of time available. While sourdough does require patience and a little bit of practice, the rewards are great, and once you get the hang of it, you will find you can slot it in around your working day, as the hands-on time is minimal. The yeasted loaves follow some of the same principles but take far less time to prove, and the quick breads, pittas, wraps and oatcakes can be made within an hour.

equipment for bread making

You can make bread without any specialist equipment, but there are a few things that will greatly improve the quality of a home-made loaf, or at the very least make your life a lot easier. You may already have a large cast-iron or heavy-based pot with a lid – if not, this is the only piece of equipment that I would recommend you invest in before you get started; the other bits you can pick up along the way. I bought all of my equipment online over the years, so there's no need to worry about finding a specialist kitchen or baking shop near you.

cast-iron/heavy-based pot

The best way to bake a sourdough loaf in a home oven is inside a cast-iron or heavy-based pot with a tightly fitting lid, as it keeps the dough moist and creates a steamy environment. I don't find that any other method works as effectively, so it is worth buying a suitable pot for this. Of course it can also be used for any other kind of stovetop cooking, so it will get plenty of use. Make sure the handle on the lid is also ovenproof. I use a Lodge or Le Creuset cast-iron pot.

proving baskets

I use 500g baskets for all the bread recipes in this book. You can buy proving baskets or bannetons for only a few pounds online – Amazon sell a number of good ones. If you become a bread-baking aficionado, then you may wish to invest in some sturdier baskets. I swear by the linen-lined baskets sold on the online retail site Bakery Bits.

If you want to test out a few breads before you buy a proving basket, then a large mixing bowl lined with a clean tea towel will be a good starting point.

razor blade or sharp knife

This is used to slash the surface of your dough just before it goes into the oven. It allows the bread to rise up dramatically, resulting in a beautiful loaf. The blade needs to be as sharp as possible, otherwise it will drag against the surface of the dough, so for this reason a razor blade or 'lame' is a handy tool, and these can be bought online very cheaply. To start with, a very sharp knife will do.

weighing scales

With any kind of baking it really helps if you can be as accurate as possible with the weights of your ingredients, particularly those that are in small quantities, as a few grams either way can have a big impact. Electric weighing scales are indispensable for any kind of cooking in my opinion, so if you don't have one I would strongly suggest putting it at the top of your birthday gift-to-yourself list.

dough scraper

This flat, blunt-edged tool is incredibly useful for scraping bits of dried-on starter or dough off your countertop, shaping your dough into a round loaf shape, or scooping up leftover flour. They only cost a few pounds online, so it's worth getting one, but you could also use a metal spatula or something similar.

pizza/baking stone

While this is by no means an essential piece of kit, if you plan on making pitta bread or pizza with any regularity, this will seriously improve the quality of the end result as the stone provides a searing heat that is not easy to achieve on a regular baking tray. Do a bit of research online before you buy anything, as you might find you have a piece of stone in your garden that is suitable!

notes on bread making

Bread making may sound like a monstrous undertaking, but I promise that once you have made a sourdough or yeasted loaf a couple of times, it is a straightforward process after that, not to mention a lifelong skill. The resulting loaf of bread is magnificent and infinitely better tasting (and cheaper) than a shop-bought loaf. Below are a few practical tips to bear in mind, and also some basic information about 'real bread' and good-quality flour.

'real' bread, and why is it so much better for you

This is bread that has been made with nothing more than flour, water, yeast and salt. The Real Bread Campaign website (www.sustainweb.org/realbread) has detailed information about what really goes into commercially made bread, including a whole range of dough conditioners, preservatives, artificial additives and enzymes, some of which are not legally required to be included on the ingredients label if they can be classified by the manufacturer as a processing aid. It is a fascinating and somewhat terrifying read, and if I have not convinced you yet to make the switch to 'real bread', then this website surely will.

baking with a variety of good-quality flours

Over the years, hybrid strains of wheat were developed in order to deliver higher yields and consistent baking results for the production of mass-produced commercial bread. As a result the density of nutrients and minerals in the grain has been affected, particularly in some of the mass-produced brands of flours. For this reason I always use organic wheat flour, and I combine it with other heritage flours such as spelt and rye. This results in a more nuanced flavour profile and an improved nutrient and mineral content.

yeast and healthy bacteria

I'm not a scientist, but I like to have a basic understanding of what is going on in my bread. I came to sourdough through making kimchi, and the fermentation process is quite similar. Essentially, wild yeasts and bacteria (known as lactobacillus) live in all flour, and when mixed with water the yeast begins to grow and multiply. Meanwhile, the lactobacillus breaks down the starch in the flour to sugars, on which they feed, converting them into lactic acid, which gives the bread its distinctive sour taste. The yeast also feed on these sugars and release bubbles of carbon dioxide, which makes the bread rise. This is only the most rudimentary of explanations, but if you are into the science of it all there is a wealth of information available online and in dedicated baking books.

kneading

For most of my bread doughs, all you have to do is stretch and fold the dough every now and again to knead it. For others, like the spelt sandwich loaf on page 54, it is a bit more hands on. If you have never kneaded before, it is a simple process. The method I like to employ is to turn the dough out on to a lightly floured work surface and, using the heel of your hand, stretch the dough away from you. Then roll the dough back in on itself, pick it up and turn it 90 degrees to your right, then stretch the dough out away from you again. Repeat this process for the time stated in the recipe, or until the dough reaches the consistency described.

dusting your proving basket

Make sure to liberally dust your proving basket, or bowl lined with a tea towel, with rice flour before putting in your dough – I can't tell you how disheartening it is to spend hours proving your dough to perfection, only to have it stick to the basket at the last minute. Rice flour is not quite as absorbent as spelt or wheat flour, so it is ideal for this task. I also find semolina works well, so I often use a combination of the two. If your dough does stick, don't fling it out the window in a fit of frustration – all is not lost. Just continue as planned; it will be a little less aesthetically pleasing, but the taste will be just as marvellous – and anyway, who's to know once it's all sliced up?

time plan for baking your sourdough loaves

Personally, I find the most time-efficient way to bake a sourdough loaf is to start on a weekend evening, finishing it off the following morning. Of course a weeknight will also be fine, as long as you have enough time in the morning (about two and a half hours) to give the dough a final rise and then bake it. The initial preparation, the evening before you bake it, takes about two hours, but the hands-on-time is only ten minutes, so you can be getting on with something else.

what is an 'active' starter?

A starter forms the basis of all sourdough breads. It is a living culture made from flour, water and wild yeasts, which helps bread to rise during baking. Making your own starter is simply a way to cultivate the wild yeasts naturally present in the flour. All you have to do is add water and let the mixture sit for a few days. Bubbles will then start forming, indicating that the wild yeasts have become active and are beginning to multiply. 'Feeding' the mixture with more flour and water helps to speed up this process. An 'active' starter means that it should be bubbly when you come to use it in your recipe. See page 22 for the recipe, and notes on how to maintain it on pages 24–25.

slashing your sourdough

Slashing your sourdough is an important step, as it enables the dramatic 'oven spring'. If you don't slash your sourdough it will still rise, breaking out and upwards through the skin of the dough. However, it may not rise as well as it would have if it were cut, so it's worth doing. It is important to approach the slashing of your dough with a degree of confidence, slashing it with a small, sharp knife in one quick and clean movement, otherwise the blade will drag against the surface of the dough. If this happens, just try again from where you left off.

sourdough starter

The starter is the foundation of any sourdough recipe. Making your own is a straightforward process – you just need to be patient. The good news is you only have to make it once, as it will last a lifetime if looked after properly. Before you begin making your starter, read the helpful tips overleaf on maintaining a healthy starter. You'll need a 500ml glass jar along with the ingredients listed below.

day 1

80g wholegrain spelt flour

20g plain white flour or white spelt flour

100ml water

2 tsp raisins

Add all the ingredients to the glass jar and thoroughly combine with a spoon. Cover loosely with the lid (so air can still circulate in and out of the jar) and leave at room temperature for 24 hours.

day 2

80g wholegrain spelt flour

20g plain white flour or white spelt flour

100ml water

Add the flours and water to the jar and combine. Cover loosely and leave at room temperature for 24 hours.

day 3

50g wholegrain spelt flour

50g plain white flour or white spelt flour

100ml water

Add the flours and water to the jar and combine. Cover loosely and leave at room temperature for 24 hours.

day 4

20g wholegrain spelt flour

80g plain white flour or white spelt flour

100ml water

Add the flours and water to the jar and combine. Cover loosely and leave at room temperature for 24 hours.

sourdough and yeasted bread

day 5

20g wholegrain spelt flour

80g plain white flour or white spelt flour

100ml water

Discard half the starter (otherwise it will be come enormous and very difficult to manage). Add the flours and water to the jar and combine. Cover loosely and leave at room temperature for 24 hours. Use an elastic band to mark the level of the starter just after you have added in the flour and water. It is then easy to see how much it is rising and falling over the course of the next 24 hours.

day 6

feeding and maintenance

100g plain white flour or white spelt flour, or a combination of the two

100ml water

From now on you will be maintaining the starter. Each day, around the same time, discard at least half the starter making sure that there is always at least 4 tablespoons remaining. Feed this remaining starter with an equal amount of flour and water. I use roughly 100g of each. Add this to the jar and combine thoroughly. Bear in mind that the amount of flour and water you add into your starter should always exceed the amount of starter you begin with. Cover loosely and leave at room temperature for 24 hours. Repeat this process of discarding and feeding every day to maintain the starter.

You will notice when you feed your starter that it doubles, and sometimes triples, in volume over the course of the following 8–12 hours. You want to use the starter when it is close to the peak of its activity. This will vary depending on the temperature of your kitchen, so just aim to feed it about 6–10 hours before you make your bread, and keep an eye on it. I like to start making my bread in the afternoon/evening after work, so I feed my starter in the morning before I leave the house and it is ready to use by the time I get home. Or, if you like to begin in the morning, just feed your starter the night before.

notes on maintaining a healthy sourdough starter

flour

The quality of the flour you use is really important to your starter. It should be the best you can find. I like to use organic, as the natural organisms present make for a happier and healthier starter. You can use a number of different flours – wheat flour is the most commonly used, but wholegrain rye flour or spelt also works well. Here I have used a combination of spelt and wheat flour.

maintaining a starter with 100 per cent spelt flour

It is possible to make a sourdough starter and loaf entirely from spelt flour, although it will not rise as dramatically as bread made with a higher percentage of wheat flour. I tend to use a combination of the two for the best result. Also, I find the gluten in spelt flour can be over-kneaded more easily than regular wheat flour, resulting in heavy, dense loaves. This is not a problem for the recipes in this book, which use the stretch and fold method, rather than vigorous kneading, but is something to bear in mind if you are using 100 per cent spelt where kneading is called for.

water

Try to use water that is as pure and natural as possible. If you have a good-quality water filter, water from that will do, or use bottled mineral water. I tend to avoid tap water as I find additives like chlorine and fluoride prevent the starter from developing properly – killing off the natural healthy bacteria necessary for growth.

what temperature should I keep my starter at?

The ideal room temperature is between 20°C and 25°C; anything higher and you may need to feed your starter more frequently, as the process speeds up dramatically. On the few occasions my kitchen exceeds 25°C I give my starter a couple of hours in the fridge every 24 hours or so, usually around midday when it is at its warmest. I have not had much experience of making sourdough in hot climates, so if you do live somewhere very warm (lucky you!), I would suggest you speak with your local baker or do further research online to find the best solution.

get to know the smell of your starter

Smell your starter throughout the day and you will quickly become familiar with the different stages the starter goes through pre- and post-feeding, from a gentle nutty sourness after being fed to a more noticeable acidity 24 hours after feeding.

pausing your starter

If you are away or only baking once or twice a week you can 'pause' your starter in the fridge. To do this, feed the starter as per the feeding and maintenance instructions (see page 23) then place it in the fridge. The day before you want to use your starter, remove it, bring it back to room temperature and feed it as per the instructions. Feed it again the following day and use it once it becomes bubbly and active. If you will not be baking again for a few days, feed the starter before returning it to the fridge. Try to feed it at least once a week. If you are going away for up to 2 weeks, feed it with double the amount of flour and a little less than double the amount of water. Anything longer than that and I would ask a friend to give it a weekly feed.

what should I do if I forget to feed my starter or if it begins to smell of alcohol?

If you forget to feed your starter for a day, feed it as soon as you remember and continue feeding it as before, every 24 hours. If you forget for more than a few days you may notice a smell of alcohol (like nail polish remover), as the starter feeds on discarded yeast and its own waste. If this happens, you can usually bring it back to life by discarding all but 3 tablespoons and feeding it with 1 tablespoon of flour. Leave for 24 hours then feed it again as per the feeding and maintenance instructions (see page 23) with equal parts flour and water. Repeat this process every 12 hours for a few days until it returns to its active bubbly state with a more neutral, slightly sweet smell.

spelt sourdough loaf

I find the most time-efficient way to bake a sourdough loaf is to start on a weekend evening, finishing it off the following morning. This recipe makes one large loaf, which is enough to last my wife and me a week. We keep some fresh, slice up the rest and freeze it, ready to be thrown into the toaster when needed. Bear in mind that if you opt for 100 per cent spelt flour, your loaves will not have the same dramatic oven spring as bread containing wheat flour, due to the lower quantities of gluten, which gives bread its structure. However, this does not affect the flavour, so if you are keen on a 100 per cent spelt flour bread don't let this fact put you off.

375ml water

75g active starter

240g wholegrain spelt flour

300g white spelt flour, or strong white bread flour

10g salt

rice flour, to dust the proving basket and work surface

1 round proving basket, or a mixing bowl lined with a clean tea towel

Ovenproof, heavy-based pot with a lid, roughly 22–24cm; a cast iron pot is ideal

step 1

In a bowl, combine the water and the starter. Don't worry if lumps remain in the starter – this is normal. In a second, larger bowl combine the flours and the salt. Add in the water and starter mixture and thoroughly mix together, ensuring there are no lumps of flour. Cover with cling film and leave at room temperature for 1 hour.

step 2

With a very lightly floured hand, to prevent sticking, stretch and fold the dough. To do this, take a portion of the dough from the base of the bowl, stretch it up and over and press it into the opposite side of the dough. Repeat this movement 4 times, turning the bowl slightly in between each movement so you work your way around the entire dough – see photos 1 to 4, pages 28–29. Cover and leave to rest for 15 minutes. Repeat this process 3 more times, leaving 15 minutes in between each kneading. The whole process should take 1 hour, but only about 2 minutes of hands-on time. Once you have finished, cover the bowl and leave it out at room temperature overnight (or for at least 8–10 hours). If you live in a very warm climate, place the bowl in the fridge overnight.

step 3

The following morning the dough should have doubled in size
and feel light and airy to the touch. If you refrigerated the dough,
remove it and leave it to prove at room temperature for a few hours
until it has doubled in size. Liberally dust your proving basket or
bowl lined with a clean tea towel with rice flour. Make sure it is
well coated, otherwise your sourdough will stick when you turn it
out into your baking vessel. (If you are following these steps for the
porridge sourdough or rye & maple sourdough, scatter the oats or
rye flakes in a thin layer on the base of your proving basket.)
Set it aside.

step 4

Lightly dust the work surface with rice flour, and gently tip the
dough out on to it. Use a spatula to help coax all the dough out, and
take care not to knock out too much air. The dough will be very soft
and a little sticky. With floured hands, take 1 edge of the dough and
pull it up and out, then back over itself into the centre of the dough.
Work your way around the dough, repeating this movement as you
go, each time pulling the edge of the dough out and then back in
over itself so that the floured edges are now all puckered together
in the centre, and the bottom surface of the dough is fully coated in
the rice flour, see step photos 5 and 6 on page 28. The dough should
feel a bit tighter at this point.

step 5

Flip the dough over so the puckered surface is facing down. Cup
your hands around the ball of dough and bring them together
underneath the dough, gently pulling the surface of the dough
downwards – see photos 7 and 8 on page 29. Rotate a little and
repeat this movement all the way around the dough until the
surface feels smooth and tight. Transfer it into your proving basket
with the smooth rice flour covered surface facing down and the
puckered surface facing up in the centre. Dust with more rice flour,
cover loosely with a tea towel and leave to rise in a warm spot for
1½ –2½ hours depending on the temperature of your kitchen, until
the dough has noticeably risen, but not doubled in size.

1

2

5

6

3

4

7

8

step 6

Thirty minutes before the final rise is complete, put your cast-iron or heavy-based pot and lid into the oven and preheat to 240°C/220°C fan/Gas mark 9.

When the final rise is completed, carefully remove the pot from the oven and gently, with the support of your hands so it does not lose its shape, invert the dough out of the basket and into the pot, so the puckered centre is now facing the bottom and the smooth surface (or oat/rye covered surface) is facing up. Take extreme care throughout this process, as the pot will be burning hot.

step 7

With a small, very sharp knife or blade, cut 2 to 4 shallow slashes into the surface of the dough, to allow the bread to expand during baking. Put the lid on the pot and place it in the oven. Immediately turn the temperature down to 220°C/200°C fan/Gas mark 7.

step 8

Bake the bread for 30 minutes, then remove the lid and bake for another 10–15 minutes, until the crust is deeply golden brown, just a few shades shy of being burnt. This is important for both texture and flavour. To check the bread is cooked through, tap the base. It should sound hollow. If not, bake for another few minutes and test again.

Once cooked, leave to cool on a wire rack. Do resist the temptation to dive in while it is still hot, as this will release all the internal steam and affect the quality of the crumb. Once it is cool enough to handle, but still warm enough to melt butter, you can go ahead and slice off a chunk of your well-earned sourdough.

kimchi sourdough

Kimchi is the reason why I first started making sourdough bread. There was something so simple and gratifying about bringing cabbage to life out of nothing really, just the natural yeasts in the air and on the vegetable – so it wasn't long before I was eager to do the same with flour and water. I use a mixture of spelt and wheat flour here – you can use all spelt flour if you prefer; the flavour will be just as good, however, as there is less gluten the bread will not have the same dramatic rise.

340ml water

20ml maple syrup

20ml kimchi juice (the liquid found at the bottom of a kimchi jar (see page 246 for cabbage and kale kimchi) or shop-bought bag)

75g active starter

100g wholegrain spelt flour

450g strong white bread flour or white spelt flour

10g salt

rice flour, to dust the proving basket and work surface

1 round proving basket, or a mixing bowl lined with a clean tea towel

Ovenproof, heavy-based pot with a lid, roughly 22–24cm; a cast iron pot is ideal

In a bowl, combine the water, maple syrup, kimchi juice and starter. Don't worry if lumps remain in the starter – this is normal.

In a second, larger bowl, combine together the flours and the salt. Add in the starter mixture and thoroughly mix together, ensuring there are no lumps of flour. Cover and leave at room temperature for 1 hour.

Continue with steps 2–8 of the spelt sourdough recipe on pages 26–27.

porridge sourdough

makes 1 loaf

I first tasted this bread at Spring restaurant in London, where my friend and former boss Skye Gyngell continues to thrill and inspire with her effortlessly delicious food. Skye came across this bread while at a workshop in the Ballymaloe Cookery School with the celebrated baker Chad Robertson, of Tartine Bakery in San Francisco, and her own version of this humble loaf has been served in her elegant restaurant ever since. I had the pleasure of going into the kitchen with Skye and her team at Spring, chatting about ferments and watching them make this 'creamy, yet chewy' bread, as Skye puts it. I have adapted the recipe so that it also works with a spelt flour combination, but the delicious chewy texture of the original remains.

for the porridge

65g rolled oats

150ml water

Pinch of sea salt

for the bread

360ml water

75g active starter

240g wholegrain bread flour or spelt flour

300g strong white bread flour or white spelt flour

13g sea salt

rice flour, to dust the proving basket and work surface

rolled oats, for coating

For the porridge, put the oats, water and a pinch of salt in a saucepan and place over a medium heat. Bring to a simmer then reduce the temperature to low and simmer gently for a few minutes, stirring all the time, until all the liquid has been absorbed and you have a thick, dry, porridge. Remove from the heat, transfer to a plate and leave to cool to room temperature. It will firm up as it cools.

In a bowl, combine the water and starter. Don't worry if lumps remain in the starter – this is normal. Add in the cooled oats and distribute into the liquid. I find my hands are the best tools for the job of squishing the thick oats into the water mixture.

In a second, larger bowl, combine the flours and the salt. Add in the water and starter mixture and thoroughly mix together, ensuring there are no lumps of flour or porridge oats. Cover and leave at room temperature for 1 hour.

1 round or oval proving basket, or a mixing bowl lined with a clean tea towel

Ovenproof, heavy-based pot with a lid, roughly 22–24cm; a cast iron pot is ideal

Continue with steps 2–8 of the spelt sourdough recipe on pages 26–30.

rye and maple sourdough

makes 1 loaf

The rye gives this sourdough an extra nuttiness that I love with the sweet maple. It lasts very well too, but will need to be toasted after a few days to get the best out of it.

330ml water

50ml maple syrup

75g active starter

100g wholegrain rye flour

450g strong white bread flour or white spelt flour

10g salt

rice flour, to dust the proving basket and work surface

rye flakes or oats for coating

1 round or oval proving basket, or a mixing bowl lined with a clean tea towel

Ovenproof, heavy-based pot with a lid, roughly 22–24cm; a cast iron pot is ideal

In a bowl, combine the water, maple syrup and starter. Don't worry if lumps remain in the starter – this is normal.

In a second, larger bowl combine the flours and the salt. Add in the water and starter mixture and thoroughly mix together, ensuring there are no lumps of flour. Cover and leave at room temperature for 1 hour.

Continue with steps 2 – 8 of the spelt sourdough recipe on page 26–30.

buckwheat, hazelnut and dried apricot sourdough

makes 1 loaf

A little buckwheat goes a long way, providing a mellow, rounded, slightly nutty flavour in this sourdough. The hazelnut and dried apricot add an unexpected crunch and sweet chewiness that I love with a little coconut oil or butter.

375ml water

75g active starter

40g buckwheat flour

100g wholegrain spelt flour

400g strong white bread flour or white spelt flour

12g salt

6 unsulphured dried apricots, roughly chopped

50g blanched hazelnuts, roasted and halved

rice flour, to dust the proving basket and work surface

1 round or oval proving basket, or a mixing bowl lined with a clean tea towel

Ovenproof, heavy-based pot with a lid, roughly 22–24cm; a cast iron pot is ideal

In a bowl, combine the water and starter. Don't worry if lumps remain in the starter – this is normal.

In a second, larger bowl combine the flours, salt, dried apricots and hazelnuts. Add in the wet mixture and thoroughly mix together, ensuring there are no lumps of flour. Cover and leave at room temperature for 1 hour.

Continue with steps 2–8 of the spelt sourdough recipe on page 26–30.

fig, almond and
cinnamon sourdough

makes 1 loaf

Feel free to mix things up and add any combination of fruit, nuts and spice to your sourdough. Just bear in mind that the quantities should be roughly the same, otherwise they will weigh down the sourdough, resulting in heavier bread.

360ml water

20ml maple syrup

75g active starter

240g wholegrain
spelt flour

300g strong white bread
flour or white spelt flour

10g salt

4 plump dried figs,
roughly chopped

40g almonds, thinly
sliced

1½ tsp ground cinnamon

rice flour, to dust the
proving basket and
work surface

1 round or oval proving
basket, or a mixing
bowl lined with a clean
tea towel

Ovenproof, heavy-based
pot with a lid, roughly
22–24cm; a cast iron
pot is ideal

In a bowl, combine the water, maple syrup and starter. Don't worry if lumps remain in the starter – this is normal.

In a second, larger bowl, combine together the flours, salt, figs, almonds and cinnamon. Add in the wet mixture and thoroughly mix together, ensuring there are no lumps of flour. Cover and leave at room temperature for 1 hour.

Continue with steps 2–8 of the spelt sourdough recipe on page 26–30.

injera

makes 2 injera

Injera is an Ethiopian fermented flatbread that I first discovered at a vegan food stall in Brick Lane years ago. It is made with teff flour (see page 167) and can be left to ferment for up to two days depending on the level of sourness that you want to come through. The hands-on time for this bread is minimal; you just have to have the forethought to get it started. It can be used as a wrap, or torn off in soft chunks to dip into soups and stews, and is also delicious as a pancake slathered with coconut oil, butter, honey or nut butter.

80g teff flour

160ml water

¼ tsp sea salt

½ tsp active dried yeast

olive oil, for frying

In a large bowl, whisk together all the ingredients, apart from the oil, until smooth. Cover and leave at room temperature for 24 hours.

After this time, spoon off any water that has risen to the top of the bowl, if any. Put 1 teaspoon olive oil in a 24cm non-stick frying pan with a lid, and set over a medium-low heat. Once hot, pour in half the batter and swirl around to form an even surface. When it begins to bubble cover with the lid and cook for 1–2 minutes, until the surface is covered in bubbles. Remove the lid and continue to cook for another 30 seconds or so, or until the surface of the flatbread is completely dry and cooked through. Remove from the heat, put the injera on a plate and cover with a clean tea towel while you cook the remaining batter. Injera goes particularly well with the puy lentil soup, page 186.

sourdough blueberry pancakes

**makes 6–8
pancakes**

These pancakes are reason enough to make your own
sourdough starter – the dense, almost chewy texture
and deep flavour simply cannot be achieved without
a fermented starter. They are seriously good.

120g active starter

100g white or
wholegrain spelt flour

65ml milk (almond,
rice or dairy)

1 egg, beaten

Pinch sea salt

1 tsp baking powder

2 tbsp extra virgin
coconut oil, plus more
to serve

100g blueberries, plus
more to serve

Maple syrup, to serve

Yoghurt (Greek, coconut
or soy, to serve, optional)

In a bowl, combine the starter, flour, milk, egg and salt.
Cover loosely and leave to one side for 20 minutes,
then stir in the baking powder.

Put 2 teaspoons of the coconut oil in a frying pan
and set it over a medium heat. Once hot add 3 level
tablespoons of the batter to the pan and shape into a
disc roughly 8cm across. Repeat with more batter, but
don't overcrowd the pan. You can use a second pan to
speed up the process if you wish.

Add 5–6 blueberries to the top of each pancake and
very gently press them into the batter. Fry for about
2 minutes, depending on the heat of the pan, then
flip over and fry for another 2–3 minutes, until golden
and caramelised.

Serve the pancakes immediately with a little more
coconut oil, blueberries, maple syrup and some
yoghurt if you like.

olive and herb yeasted bread

This yeasted bread follows the same steps as the sourdough breads, but without the overnight rise, so if you are short on time but still want a beautiful big loaf, this is the one to go for. You can play around with the flavouring ingredients here too – the possibilities are endless.

380ml warm water

1 x 7g sachet of fast-action dried yeast

1 tsp honey or maple syrup

100g wholegrain spelt flour

450g strong white bread flour or white spelt flour

10g salt

50g black pitted olives, sliced

50g green pitted olives, sliced

2 tsp mixed dried herbs

rice flour, to dust the proving basket and work surface

1 round or oval proving basket, or a mixing bowl lined with a clean tea towel

Ovenproof, heavy-based pot with a lid, roughly 22–24cm; a cast iron pot is ideal

step 1

Combine the water, yeast and honey or maple syrup in a bowl and set aside for 10 minutes, until frothy.

step 2

In a second, larger bowl, combine the flours and salt. Add in the yeast and water, olives and herbs and thoroughly mix together, ensuring there are no lumps of flour. Cover and leave at room temperature for 1 hour.

step 3

With a very lightly floured hand to prevent sticking, stretch and fold the dough. To do this, take a portion of the dough from the base of the bowl, stretch it up and over and press it into the opposite side of the dough. Repeat this movement 4 times, turning the bowl slightly in between each movement so you work your way around the entire dough, see photos 1–4 on pages 28–29. Cover and leave to rest for 15 minutes.

step 4

Repeat this process 3 more times, leaving 15 minutes in between each folding. The whole process should take 1 hour, but involves only a few minutes of hands-on time. Once you have finished, cover the bowl loosely and leave to rise in a warm spot until the dough doubles in size.

step 5

Liberally dust the proving basket or bowl lined with a clean tea towel with rice flour. Make sure it is well coated, otherwise your dough will stick when you turn it out into your baking vessel. Set it aside.

step 6

Once the dough has doubled in size, dust the work surface with rice flour and tip the dough out on to it. With floured hands, take 1 edge of the dough and pull it up and back in over itself into the centre of the dough. Work your way around the dough, repeating this movement as you go, each time pulling the edge of the dough out and then back in over itself so that the floured edges are now all puckered together in the centre, and the bottom surface of the dough is smooth and coated in the rice flour, see photos 5–6 on pages 28. The dough should feel a bit tighter at this point.

step 7

Flip the dough over so the puckered surface is facing down, cup your hands around the ball of dough and bring them together underneath the dough, gently pulling the surface of the dough downwards. Rotate a little and repeat this movement all the way around the dough until the surface feels smooth and tight see photos 7–8 on page 29. Transfer the dough to the proving basket with the smooth surface facing down and the puckered surface facing up in the centre. Dust with a little more rice flour, cover loosely and leave to rise in a warm spot for 40–60 minutes, or until the dough has noticeably risen.

step 8

Thirty minutes before the final rise is complete, put your cast-iron or heavy-based pot and lid into the oven and preheat to 240°C/220°C fan/Gas mark 9.

step 9

When the final rise is completed, carefully remove the pot from the oven and gently, with the support of your hands so it does not lose its shape, invert the dough out of the basket and into the pot, so the puckered centre is now facing the bottom. Take extreme care throughout this process, as the pot will be burning hot.

step 10

With a small, very sharp knife or blade, cut 2 to 4 shallow slashes into the surface of the dough, to allow the bread to expand during baking. Put the lid on the pot and place it in the oven. Immediately turn the temperature down to 220°C/200°C fan/Gas mark 7.

step 11

Bake the bread for 30 minutes, then remove the lid and bake for another 10–15 minutes, until the crust is a deep golden brown. To check the bread is cooked through, tap the base. It should sound hollow. If not, bake for another few minutes and test again.

Once cooked, transfer to a wire rack and leave to cool before slicing.

rye, pecan and date loaf

makes 1 loaf

Earthy rye and sweet dates are the perfect match here, and combined with the pecans they make this an excellent breakfast loaf.

380ml warm water

1 x 7g sachet of fast-action dried yeast

1 tsp honey or maple syrup

100g rye flour

450g strong white bread flour or white spelt flour

10g salt

60g pecan nuts, sliced

7 dates, pitted and chopped

rice flour, to dust the proving basket and work surface

1 round or oval proving basket, or a mixing bowl lined with a clean tea towel

Ovenproof, heavy-based pot with a lid, roughly 22–24cm; a cast iron pot is ideal

Combine the water, yeast and honey or maple syrup in a bowl and set aside for 10 minutes, until frothy.

In a second, larger bowl, combine the flours, salt, pecans and dates. Add in the yeast and water and thoroughly mix together, ensuring there are no lumps of flour. Cover and leave at room temperature for 1 hour.

Continue with steps 3–11 from the olive and herb bread recipe on pages 46–48.

black multigrain seed bread

This is similar to rye bread, but with a lot more going on – it's packed full of grains and seeds, so is nourishing and wholesome in the best kind of way. It is also very moist, so you don't feel like you're trying to force down a slice of cardboard for breakfast. I love to slather over some coconut oil, tahini and jam – this may sound like an odd combination, but I urge you to try it.

100g rye grains

100g spelt or wheat grains

50g sunflower seeds

50g pumpkin seeds

50g linseeds

10g salt

280ml warm water

250g white spelt flour (or 125g each of wholegrain spelt flour and white spelt flour)

100g rye flour

1 tbsp maple syrup

2 tbsp cocoa powder

1 tbsp extra virgin olive oil or melted extra virgin coconut oil

150ml warm water

50g yoghurt (Greek, soy or coconut)

1 tsp fast-action yeast

2 tsp black and white sesame seeds

23cm x 13cm loaf tin

Lightly grease the loaf tin and line with baking parchment. Make sure your loaf tin is at least the size of the given measurements, otherwise the dough may spill out when proving.

Put a saucepan of water on to boil. Add in the rye and spelt or wheat grains, return to the boil, then reduce the heat and simmer for 30–40 minutes, until the grains are just cooked through but are still chewy with a bit of a bite to them. Drain off the water completely, then put the hot dry grains in a large bowl together with all the seeds and salt. Cover with 280ml of water and leave to one side for about 1 hour until the mixture is gelatinous.

Add the rest of the ingredients apart from the sesame seeds, and thoroughly combine, mixing for a few minutes by hand (or you can use a stand mixer). Transfer the mixture to the loaf tin and press it into the corners with a wet spoon, flattening the top. Scatter over the sesame seeds, cover with cling film and leave to rise in a warm spot in your kitchen for 1½–2 hours, or until the dough has noticeably risen above the edges of the loaf tin.

About half an hour before the dough has fully risen, preheat the oven to 190°C/170°C fan/Gas mark 5.

Discard the cling film and bake for 1 hour. Remove from the tin, return to the oven and bake for a further 10–15 minutes to achieve a firm crust. Remove and leave to cool completely before slicing.

spelt sandwich loaf

makes 1 loaf

This is the bread to make if you're hankering after a traditional loaf for sandwiches and toast. The kind of bread your grandparents might have had, wrapped in brown paper on the kitchen counter.

400g white spelt flour, plus extra for kneading

200g wholegrain spelt flour

10g salt

2 tsp honey or maple syrup

1 x 7g sachet of fast-action dried yeast

30ml olive oil, plus extra for greasing

400ml water

spelt flakes or oats, to sprinkle over (optional)

1 large loaf tin measuring 23cm x 13cm, greased

Place all the ingredients, apart from the spelt flakes or oats, into a large mixing bowl and combine with a wooden spoon, until no dry flour remains visible. Cover loosely and leave to one side for 10 minutes.

Turn the dough out on to a lightly floured surface and knead for 5 minutes (as described on page 19). Stop and leave the dough to rest for 2 minutes, then knead again for another 5 minutes. Repeat this step 1 more time so you have kneaded the dough for a total of 15 minutes. It should be elastic and stretchy with a smooth sheen to it. (If you are using an electric stand mixer, the kneading time can be halved.) The dough may be a little sticky at first, but this will change as you knead, so don't be tempted to add too much extra flour. Place the dough in a large bowl, cover lightly and leave to prove for 1 hour, or until doubled in size.

Fold the dough in on itself a few times to knock out all the air. Tip the dough out on to a lightly floured surface. Flatten it into a rough oblong and fold the top left-hand and right-hand corners in on themselves. Swivel it around and do the same with the other 2 corners, until the dough is roughly the shape and size of your loaf tin.

Flip the dough over so the puckered surface is facing down, cradle the dough with your hands and continue to shape the dough into a rough oval/rectangle, pulling the edges of the dough down and underneath itself to tighten the surface. Transfer the dough to the greased tin, making sure the puckered surface is facing down and the smooth surface is facing up. Brush with a little water and sprinkle over some spelt flakes, or oats if using. Cover loosely and leave to rise for another 35–55 minutes, until noticeably bigger, but not quite doubled in size.

Place a baking tray in the base of the oven and preheat it to 240°C/ 220°C fan/Gas mark 9. When the dough has risen, place the loaf tin on a shelf in the oven, pour a cup of cold water into the hot baking tray and close the door immediately. Turn the temperature down to 220°C/200°C fan/Gas mark 7 and bake for 35 minutes, until golden. Remove the loaf from its tin and return it to the oven for a further 10–15 minutes, until it is deep golden brown and the base sounds hollow when lightly tapped with your finger. Leave to cool completely on a wire rack. If you want a very soft crust, keep the bread covered with a damp tea towel.

gluten-free sandwich loaf

makes 1 loaf

Creating a gluten-free bread can be tricky, particularly if you are trying to make something similar to a sourdough. However, it is possible to make a perfectly acceptable sandwich loaf at home. The technique is completely different as the absence of gluten means that kneading is not required. The consistency of the dough will also seem very wet, but stick with it and you will be rewarded with a light and moist loaf perfect for making sandwiches and toast.

365ml warm water

1 tbsp honey or
maple syrup

14g active dried yeast

375g gluten-free
flour mix

1½ tsp xanthan gum

1 tsp baking powder

1 tsp bicarbonate of soda

1½ tsp fine sea salt

1½ tsp lemon juice

4 tbsp olive oil

2 eggs

21cm x 10cm loaf tin

Preheat the oven to 200°C/180°C fan/Gas mark 6, and grease and line the base of the loaf tin.

In a bowl, combine the warm water, honey or maple syrup and dried yeast. Leave to one side until frothy.

Sieve the gluten-free flour mix, xanthan gum, baking powder, bicarbonate of soda and salt into a large bowl, and combine. Once the water and yeast mixture has frothed up a little, add in the lemon juice, olive oil and eggs and whisk to combine. Pour all but two tablespoons of the mixture into the flour and thoroughly combine, mixing until smooth. Sometimes the flour will hold moisture from the air and will therefore need a little less liquid than the recipe makes. So add in the remaining 2 tablespoons of liquid bit by bit until the mixture is wet and sticky, but not overly sloppy – it should hold its shape a little.

Using a spatula, scrape the mixture into the loaf tin and smooth out the surface with the back of a spoon dipped in water; don't worry if it appears very wet. Set aside for 15 minutes in a warm spot.

Bake for 50 minutes, until golden brown with a firm crust. Remove from the tin and cook on its side for a further 10 minutes. To test if it is cooked through, tap the base gently; it should sound hollow. If the bread looks like it is going to burn on the outside, cover it with foil and continue to bake until it is done.

Remove from the oven and leave to cool completely on a wire rack. Don't attempt to slice the bread while it' still warm, as is it will crumble.

spelt and poppy seed pitta

makes 10 pittas

Making pitta bread is surprisingly straightforward. These are most delicious fresh from the oven, so the best thing to do is make the dough whenever you have time, then cover and refrigerate for up to a week. You can then bake fresh pitta in record time. Alternatively, you can bake them all in advance and freeze them, then all you have to do is pop them in the toaster at the last moment.

1½ tsp of fast-action dried yeast

190ml warm water (not hot or boiling)

1 tsp honey or maple syrup

300g white spelt flour, plus extra to dust

1 tbsp poppy seeds

1 tsp extra virgin olive oil

1½ tsp fine sea salt

In a large bowl, mix together the yeast, warm water and honey or maple syrup. Leave to one side for 10–15 minutes, until frothy.

Add the flour, poppy seeds, olive oil and salt and combine to form a rough dough. Knead the dough for 8–10 minutes by hand, until smooth and elastic. If you are using a stand mixer it will take roughly half the time. Place the dough in a bowl, cover and leave to rise in a warm spot for 1½–2 hours, or until doubled in size. At this point the dough can be covered and refrigerated for up to 1 week, ready to make fresh pitta whenever you want.

If you want to cook them all now, 30 minutes before the dough has finished proving, preheat the oven to its highest temperature setting, ideally 240°C/220°C fan/ Gas mark 9. Put a heavy-based baking tray or a pizza stone into the oven to preheat as well. Bear in mind that it is crucial to fully preheat the oven and baking tray/stone at the highest temperature, otherwise the pittas may not puff up properly.

Once the dough has risen, turn it out on to a lightly floured surface and divide it into 10 pieces of equal size. Roll each piece into a ball, dust a rolling pin with a little flour and roll each ball into a thin round, measuring 14–16cm across. Dust with a little flour as you go to ensure the pittas don't stick.

To bake, place as many pittas as you can onto the baking tray or pizza stone and cook for 2–4 minutes until they have puffed up completely. Remove and cover with a clean tea towel while you cook the remaining dough. To freeze the pittas, leave them to cool completely, transfer them to a resealable freezer bag with a layer of baking parchment in between each one, and freeze until needed.

spelt wraps

makes 6 wraps

These can be made at the last minute for a speedy breakfast wrap or a packed lunch, or as a tortilla for a quick quesadilla. It is also delicious drizzled with good extra virgin olive oil and a sprinkling of sea salt!

200g white or wholegrain spelt flour, or a mixture of both, plus extra to dust

½ tsp fine sea salt

2 tbsp extra virgin olive oil

100ml water

In a large bowl, combine the flour and salt. Add the oil and all but 1 or 2 tablespoons of the water, and bring the mixture together into a dough. Add the remaining water a bit at a time to form a smooth, soft dough – it should not be sticky. Knead for 2 minutes just to make sure everything is well combined. Cover and set aside for 15 minutes to rest.

Divide the dough into 6 pieces of equal size. One by one roll the dough into a ball, dust the work surface with flour and roll each ball out into a thin round measuring about 22cm across. Dust with flour as you go to ensure the dough does not stick.

Place a non-stick frying pan over a low–medium heat, add the wrap and cook for about 40 seconds on each side, until just cooked through. Place on a plate and immediately cover with a clean tea towel. Use straight away, or freeze with a sheet of baking parchment in between each wrap.

sourdough and yeasted bread

super-fast, no-knead spelt and rye loaf

makes 1 loaf

This loaf is for the days when you are short on time, or have realised too late that only one slice of your beloved sourdough remains! It comes together in a flash and requires no kneading or proving time – you just fire it into the oven and an hour later you have a beautiful loaf, somewhere between an Irish soda bread and a country loaf. Feel free to play around with the flours a little, and any number of herbs, seeds, dried fruits and nuts can be added to it.

200g wholegrain spelt flour

200g white spelt flour, or more wholegrain if you prefer

100g rye flour

1 tsp baking powder

1 tsp bicarbonate of soda

1 tsp sea salt

80g pumpkin seeds

40g sunflower seeds

80g raisins (optional)

1 tbsp blackstrap molasses or maple syrup

520ml tepid water

23cm x 13cm loaf tin

Preheat the oven to 200°C/180°C fan/Gas mark 6, and lightly grease the loaf tin and line it with baking parchment.

Thoroughly mix all the dry ingredients together in a bowl, then add the molasses and water and mix again until just combined.

Pour into the loaf tin and bake for 50 minutes, then carefully remove the loaf from its tin and continue to bake on its side for a further 10 minutes.

Remove the loaf from the oven and leave to cool completely before cutting.

chia oatcakes

**makes 20–25
oatcakes**

We fly through these at home – they are the perfect
little snack, and work well with just about any
topping. A particular guilty pleasure of mine is a light
slathering of coconut oil and nut butter topped with
a Medjool date and a tiny sprinkling of sea salt. It's
basically a mini Medjool date tart. Too good!

200g fine oatmeal

35g wholegrain spelt
flour, plus extra to dust

15g chia seeds

1 tsp fine sea salt

¼ tsp bicarbonate
of soda

20ml olive oil or melted
extra virgin coconut oil

90–95ml hot water

Preheat the oven to 190°C/170°C fan/Gas mark 5,
and line 2 baking sheets with baking parchment.

In a large bowl, combine the oatmeal, flour, chia
seeds, salt and bicarbonate of soda. Add the olive
oil or melted coconut oil and 90–95ml of hot water.
Combine until everything comes together into a ball
of dough. If it is still crumbly, add a few more drops
of water.

Dust the work surface with a little flour. Flatten the
ball of dough and roll out to 4–5mm thickness, dusting
with extra flour as you go to make sure the underside
of the dough does not stick to the work surface. Cut
out the oatcakes with your preferred biscuit cutters
and transfer them to the baking sheets.

Bake for 20–25 minutes, until the edges of the
oatcakes are golden. Leave to cool for 10 minutes
on the baking sheets, then carefully transfer them to
a wire rack to cool completely. Store in an airtight
container for up to 1 week.

spiced crispbreads

makes 4 large cripsbreads

These wafer-thin cripsbreads are a good way to start any kind of meal, with some labneh (see page 216) or hummus, or simply drizzle over some grassy extra virgin olive oil. They can be topped with any of your favourite spices and seeds too – the possibilities are endless.

100g white or wholegrain spelt flour, plus extra to dust

25g rye flour

¾ tsp fast-action dry yeast

½ tsp sea salt, plus extra to sprinkle over

1½ tsp honey

70ml warm water (not hot or boiling)

optional toppings

Cumin seeds, chili flakes, oregano, etc.

Put all the ingredients in a bowl and knead for 1–2 minutes, until everything is well combined and you have a ball of dough. Cover and leave to rest for 1 hour at room temperature.

20 minutes before the resting time is finished, preheat the oven to 210°C/190°C fan/Gas mark 7 and line two baking sheets with baking parchment.

Knead the dough one or twice to knock out the air, then divide into four equal-sized pieces. Dust the work surface with flour and roll out each piece of dough as thinly as possible, turning and flipping the dough as you roll, and dusting with more flour as necessary to ensure it doesn't stick. Don't worry about the shape of the dough, as the crispbreads will be broken into shards once baked. Carefully transfer the wafer-thin sheet to the baking tray and repeat with the remaining pieces of dough. You will need one baking tray per sheet of dough – or bake in batches.

Using a fork, prick holes all over the dough sheets. Brush the surface of the dough with a small amount of water, then sprinkle over some sea salt and any other spices and herbs you like. Bake for 5–7 minutes, until the dough is golden and crisp, keeping a close eye on the crispbreads as they burn quickly.

sourdough and yeasted bread

Leave to cool, then transfer to a wire rack to cool completely. Break into irregular shards and serve with any dip you like, or simply with really good extra virgin olive oil. Store in an airtight container for up to 1 week.

sweet
baking

There are so many ways
to make sweet baking that
little bit more nourishing
and wholesome – with
interesting flours, spices,
nuts and fruit. All of the
recipes in this chapter offer
alternatives to dairy and
avoid cane sugar; however,
they are still very much an
indulgent treat – everything
in moderation, and all that.

italian strawberry and chocolate chunk cake

serves 8

My wife and I ate a cake in a café in Milan that had monstrous chunks of chocolate suspended within its sponge. I asked the owner and chef how she managed to prevent such enormous lumps of chocolate from sinking to the bottom of the cake – but she refused to let me in on her trade secret! I have settled for slightly smaller chunks, but still far bigger than chocolate chips, and these are layered into the cake with the strawberries. When the cake cools the chocolate sets a little, so you have moist pools of strawberry beside chewy, rich chocolate. There really is nothing not to like about this cake.

4 eggs

180g flavourless extra virgin coconut oil or unsalted butter

200ml honey or maple syrup

150g ground almonds

150g white spelt flour

zest of ½ unwaxed lemon

2 tsp vanilla extract

1 tsp bicarbonate of soda

1 tsp baking powder

½ tsp fine sea salt

150g dark chocolate, minimum 70% cocoa solids, plus extra to drizzle (optional)

250g strawberries, hulled and halved, plus extra to serve (optional)

20cm spring form cake tin

Preheat the oven to 180°C/160°C fan/Gas mark 4, and grease and line the cake tin.

Put the eggs into the bowl of a stand mixer and whisk on high speed for 4–5 minutes, until they have thickened and increased in volume. Melt the coconut oil or butter in a saucepan over a low heat. Transfer the oil or butter to a bowl and stir in the honey, ground almonds, flour, lemon zest, vanilla extract, bicarbonate of soda, baking powder and salt. Fold in the whipped eggs until just combined.

Pour half of the mixture into the cake tin. Break half of the chocolate into large thumb-sized chunks and position them on top of the batter. Do the same with half of the strawberries, then top with the remaining cake batter and top with the remaining chocolate and strawberries as you did before. Bake for 1 hour and 15 minutes, until the cake feels firm to the touch and springs back under gentle pressure.

If it is browning too quickly, cover with foil and continue cooking. Leave to cool for 15 minutes, then turn out on to a wire rack to cool completely.

Serve the cake as it is, or go the whole hog and top with some more fresh strawberries and drizzle over some melted chocolate.

parsnip cake

The addition of parsnip to a cake always seems to draw gasps, but it is no more unusual than the addition of carrot. In fact I would argue that the chewy sweetness of parsnips makes them even more of a kindred spirit to a dense and moist sponge cake – but I will let you be the judge of that.

200g white spelt flour

50g rye flour, or more spelt flour

2 tsp bicarbonate of soda

1 tsp baking powder

1½ tsp ground cinnamon

1½ tsp mixed spice

¼ tsp sea salt

3 eggs

230ml milk (dairy, rice or almond)

2 tbsp lemon juice

180ml mild rapeseed oil or melted extra virgin coconut oil

260g coconut palm sugar

2 tsp vanilla extract

220g coarsely grated parsnip

180g desiccated coconut

100g raisins

2 tsp extra virgin coconut oil

75g toasted flaked almonds

2 tsp maple syrup

For the icing, put the cream cheese and honey into a food processor and pulse on and off until combined; don't overmix. Put the mixture into a bowl, and stir in the melted coconut oil and lemon zest. Cover and refrigerate while you make the cake.

Preheat the oven to 200°C/180°C fan/Gas mark 6. Grease and line the cake tin.

In a bowl, sift together the flours, bicarbonate of soda, baking powder, cinnamon, mixed spice and salt. In another bowl combine the eggs, milk, lemon juice, 180ml oil, sugar and vanilla extract. Add in the flour mixture, grated parsnip, desiccated coconut and raisins, and thoroughly combine.

Pour the mixture into the tin, cover with foil and bake for 30 minutes, remove the foil and bake for a further 25–35 minutes, until a skewer comes out mostly clean and the cake is firm to the touch. Remove the cake from the oven, leave to cool for 10 minutes then turn out on to a wire rack until completely cool.

icing

250g cream cheese or a dairy-free cream cheese alternative

3 tbsp set honey

40g extra virgin coconut oil, melted

zest of 2 lemons

23cm round springform cake tin

For the almond topping, put the 2 teaspoons of coconut oil into a pan and set over a medium heat. Add the toasted flaked almonds and maple syrup and fry for 2 minutes, until the almonds are coated and glossy. Remove from the heat and leave to cool.

When the cake is cool, spread the icing over the top then scatter over the almonds.

peach, pistachio and coconut cake

serves 8

This is a summer cake to be made on those (all too rare) long, balmy evenings when one could imagine, if only for the briefest of moments, that the summer might never end. Windows and doors flung open, radio on, this comes together in no time at all. Dense and moist and rich with the ripe summer juices of the peaches, this cake longs for a dollop of yoghurt or ice cream. Feel free to swap in pretty much any stone fruit, and ground almonds work just as well if you find yourself without pistachios.

100g shelled pistachio nuts, or ground almonds, raw and unsalted

150g extra virgin coconut oil or unsalted butter

150g coconut palm sugar

2 tsp vanilla extract

Zest of 1 unwaxed lemon

3 eggs, beaten

125g white spelt flour

50g desiccated coconut, plus extra to serve

2 tsp baking powder

3–4 peaches, halved and stoned

yoghurt (dairy, coconut or soy, to serve)

20cm round springform cake tin

Preheat the oven to 180°C/160°C fan/Gas mark 4, and grease and line the cake tin.

Put the pistachios in a food processor and blitz to a rough powder, taking care not to go too far, or they will turn into a paste. Transfer the powder to a bowl. If using ground almonds, skip this step.

Add the coconut oil or butter, coconut palm sugar, vanilla and lemon zest to the processor, and blitz until combined and light. Add the eggs and blitz briefly, until the mixture comes together. Place the mixture in a large bowl and fold in the flour, a little at a time, until thoroughly combined. Fold in the ground pistachios or almonds, desiccated coconut and baking powder.

Pour the mixture into the cake tin. Gently top with the peach halves, flesh side down, and bake for 40–50 minutes, until golden brown and a skewer inserted into the centre comes out clean. If it is browning too quickly, cover with foil. Remove and leave to cool completely before serving, with yoghurt if you like.

gluten-free chocolate, buckwheat and cardamom cake

serves 8–10

I have included 'gluten free' in this title simply because it makes it easier to find for those people who are coeliac or following a gluten-free diet. However, the fact there is no gluten is completely beside the point; first and foremost this is an incredibly moist, dense and indulgent cake. Buckwheat, despite the name, is not wheat at all – and a little goes a long way, but it adds a nice nutty flavour here. I love cardamom, but if you are not keen on it just leave it out; the intense chocolate flavour is wonderful as it is.

120g dark chocolate, minimum 70% cocoa solids

120g extra virgin coconut oil or unsalted butter

120g coconut palm sugar

4 eggs

good pinch of sea salt

120g blanched almonds

40g buckwheat flour, or spelt flour if you can tolerate gluten

½ tsp ground cardamom

2 tsp vanilla extract

1 tsp bicarbonate of soda

1 tsp baking powder

icing

300g cream cheese or a dairy-free cream cheese alternative

4 tbsp set honey

Preheat the oven to 180°C/160°C fan/Gas mark 4, and grease and line the 2 cake tins.

For the icing, put the cream cheese and honey into a food processor and blitz until smooth. Transfer to a bowl and stir through the melted coconut oil. Cover and refrigerate.

Melt the chocolate and coconut oil or butter in a heatproof bowl set over a pan of barely simmering water. In a separate bowl, whisk the sugar, eggs and salt together until the mixture has increased in volume and is light. Put the almonds into a food processor and blitz to a rough powder, but don't worry if there are a few larger chunks – this adds to the texture and flavour. Stir the almonds, flour, cardamom, vanilla extract, bicarbonate of soda and baking powder into the chocolate mixture, then fold in the egg and sugar mixture until well combined. It is quite a wet mixture, but this is fine.

100g extra virgin
coconut oil, melted

cocoa powder, to dust

2 x 18cm round cake
tins

Divide the mixture between the 2 cake tins and bake for 20–25
minutes, until the sides of the cake are firm and cooked through,
but the very centre remains a little unset. This will firm up as it
cools and will ensure a really moist and squidgy cake. Remove from
the oven and leave to cool for 15 minutes, then carefully turn out
on to a wire rack and leave to cool completely.

Ice 1 layer with half the icing, place the second layer on top and
finish with the remaining icing. Dust liberally with cocoa powder,
and serve.

chocolate, cinnamon and pecan babka

makes 1 loaf

I was invited to watch the recording of the Martha Stewart Show when I was living in New York years ago. The whole experience was hilarious, but one moment that stuck with me was hearing Martha talk passionately with one of her guests about her 'babka' recipe. I had no idea what a babka was at the time, but was dying to try it out after hearing her description – and it absolutely does not disappoint. Martha's version is rammed with butter and cane sugar, and it does taste incredible, but I recently developed this version for a friend who can't eat dairy and it is just as indulgent and delicious. This is time-consuming to make as it is a yeasted cake which requires overnight proving, but the results are really special – a beautiful twisted dough with pools of chocolate nuttiness in the centre. Despite appearances it is also relatively straightforward; just follow the instructions carefully and you will be rewarded.

75ml milk (dairy, rice or almond)

2½ tsp fast-action dried yeast

310g white spelt flour, plus extra to dust

60g coconut palm sugar

¼ tsp sea salt

1 egg, beaten

80g extra virgin coconut oil or unsalted butter, melted

cont.

Warm the milk in a pan until just tepid. Remove from the heat, add the yeast and set to one side for 10 minutes, until frothy.

Put the flour, sugar and salt into the bowl of an electric mixer fitted with a dough hook. Mix in the egg, the milk and yeast mixture and the melted coconut oil or butter until it all comes together into a ball of dough. Continue to knead for 8–10 minutes on medium speed, until the dough is shiny, soft and smooth. Sprinkle in a small amount of spelt flour every now and again to help the dough lift away from the side of the bowl. Leave at room temperature for 30 minutes, then cover and refrigerate overnight. This can also be done by hand, but it will take a little longer to knead.

filling

100g dark chocolate, minimum 70% cocoa solids

20g cocoa powder

150g coconut palm sugar

1½ tsp ground cinnamon or ½ tsp ground cardamom

pinch of sea salt

60g extra virgin coconut oil or unsalted butter

70g pecans, lightly roasted at 180°C until they are a shade darker

100ml maple syrup

21cm x 10cm loaf tin

The next day, grease and line the loaf tin.

To make the filling, melt the chocolate in a heatproof bowl set over a pan of barely simmering water. Remove it from the heat and stir in the cocoa powder, coconut palm sugar, cinnamon or ground cardamom, salt and coconut oil or butter until the sugar has dissolved and the oil or butter has melted into the mixture.

Put 50g of the pecans into a food processor and blitz to a rough powder. Add this to the chocolate mixture and leave to cool until the mixture is thick. It should be spreadable and sticky, but not too loose. Roughly chop the remaining pecan nuts.

Lightly dust the work surface with flour and roll the dough out into a rectangle shape, measuring roughly 36cm x 26cm. The dough will be quite firm from the fridge, but just keep working it into a rectangle shape with your hands and a rolling pin, and don't worry if the edges are not perfectly straight – you won't notice once it's assembled and baked. Spread the chocolate mixture over the dough, leaving a 1cm border around the edge. Sprinkle over the remaining nuts.

Roll the dough tightly, from one long side to the other, as you would when making sushi, to form a thick cigar shape roughly 36cm long. With both hands, even out the dough into a smooth log. With a sharp knife, cut the log in half lengthways, from top to bottom, so that you have 2 perfectly even long halves, with the layers of dough and chocolate facing up. If the dough feels too soft to handle, put it in the fridge for 15–20 minutes to firm up. If it still feels firm enough, you can begin to plait the dough. Press together the tips of the 2 lengths of dough. Now begin crossing 1 length of dough over the other, working your way down the lengths of dough, until both pieces are fully intertwined, then press the 2 pieces together at the bottom, as you did at the top. Don't worry too much if it is a bit messy or the layers of dough begin to open out, just push them back together gently.

Carefully transfer the entire plait into the loaf tin. You will need to tuck the ends of the plait underneath themselves in order for them to fit in the tin. Place the babka in a warm place and leave it to prove for 1½–2 hours, until the dough has risen and become soft. It will not double in size, but this is fine. If your kitchen is cold, you may need to place it near a radiator, as it does require a warm spot to rise properly.

About 30 minutes before the babka has finished proving, preheat the oven to 200°C/180°C fan/Gas mark 6. Bake the babka for about 30–35 minutes, until golden. A skewer should glide in without resistance. If it is undercooked the skewer will stick a bit in places. If it is browning too quickly, cover with foil and continue.

Remove from the oven and immediately pour over the maple syrup, covering the whole loaf. Leave the loaf to cool and absorb the maple syrup, then remove it from the tin and serve in thick slices.

sweet shortcrust pastry

250g white spelt flour, plus extra to dust

¼ tsp fine sea salt

120g flavourless extra virgin coconut oil or unsalted butter, chilled and cut into small pieces

1 tbsp maple syrup

Preheat the oven to 200°C/180°C fan/Gas mark 6.

Sift the flour and salt into the bowl of a food processor. Add the chilled coconut oil or butter, and blitz until the mixture resembles fine breadcrumbs. Add the maple syrup and 1½–2 of tablespoons water and bring the dough together with your hands until you have a smooth ball. If it is still crumbly, add a few drops of water, being careful not to overdo it. Flatten the ball, wrap it in cling film and refrigerate for 30 minutes until well chilled but still pliable.

Once the pastry has chilled, roll it out between 2 sheets of floured cling film and line your tart tin. If you find the pastry too difficult to handle, simply press the pastry directly into the tin, making sure the base and sides are smooth and even with no cracks. Cover and chill the base in the freezer for 10 minutes. Prick the base all over with a fork, line with baking parchment, fill with baking beans, and blind bake for 20 minutes. Remove the parchment and beans and bake for a further 5 minutes, until the tart shell is cooked through and biscuity. Continue with the rest of the recipe.

gluten-free pastry

250g gluten-free flour mix

¼ tsp fine sea salt

¼ tsp xanthan gum

120g flavourless extra virgin coconut oil or unsalted butter, chilled and cut into small pieces

1 tbsp maple syrup

Follow the same method as above, adding the xanthan gum to the flour and salt mixture.

chocolate pastry

225g white spelt flour

25g cocoa powder

½ tsp fine sea salt

120g flavourless extra virgin coconut oil or unsalted butter, chilled and cut into small pieces

1 tbsp maple syrup

Preheat the oven to 200°C/180°C fan/Gas mark 6.

Sift the flour, cocoa powder and salt into the bowl of a food processor, then proceed with the sweet shortcrust pastry method on the opposite page.

hazelnut coconut caramel tart

serves 12

Making a caramel without dairy or cane sugar that was just as unctuous and deeply flavoured as the original took a bit of testing to get right, and in the end it was the simplest combination of coconut cream and coconut palm sugar that did it. Here it is combined with whole hazelnuts to create a truly decadent tart.

1 quantity of sweet
shortcrust pastry
(see page 86)

filling

400g blanched
hazelnuts

350ml coconut cream

200g coconut
palm sugar

½ tsp sea salt

75g extra virgin coconut
oil or unsalted butter

1 tsp vanilla extract

6 egg yolks

to serve

yoghurt (Greek,
coconut or soy),
or ice cream

Preheat the oven to 200°C/180°C fan/Gas mark 6.

Make the pastry case according to the method on page 86.

Spread out the hazelnuts on a baking tray and bake for 5–6 minutes, until they are a shade darker and aromatic. Leave to cool.

For the filling, put the coconut cream and coconut palm sugar into a saucepan over a medium–high heat. Bring to the boil, then reduce the heat, add the sea salt and simmer briskly for 10–15 minutes, stirring frequently, until you have a viscous caramel. You should be able to draw a line through it with a wooden spoon. Remove and set aside to cool.

Put all but 2 tablespoons of the caramel into the bowl of a food processor, together with the coconut oil or butter and the vanilla extract. Blitz, then add the egg yolks and blitz again until just combined.

Combine the caramel mixture and the hazelnuts and tip them into the blind-baked tart shell. Bake for 35–40 minutes, until the filling is set and golden brown. Cover with foil if it browns too quickly. Remove from the oven and leave to cool for 15 minutes before taking the tart out of the tin and moving it to a cooling rack to cool to room temperature.

Serve with a liberal dollop of yoghurt or ice cream, with the remaining caramel drizzled over. You may need to warm the caramel to get it to pouring consistency.

apricot tartlets

makes 6 tartlets

A lot of people think tartlets are fiddly to make, but actually they are a little easier than tarts as you don't have to bother with blind baking the pastry base. They also look beautiful, and each one is the perfect size for an individual portion, so I usually make them if we are having friends over for dinner.

1 quantity of sweet
shortcrust pastry
(see page 86)

filling

70g extra virgin
coconut oil

80g white spelt flour

50g coconut palm sugar

60g rolled oats or
coarse oatmeal

40g ground almonds

zest of 1 unwaxed
lemon

4 tbsp maple syrup

6 apricots, or about
4 peaches or nectarines,
halved and stoned

handful of redcurrants
(optional), plus extra
to serve

3 tbsp apricot jam, to
glaze (I find the French
St Dalfour sugar-free
jams the best; they are
sweetened only with
natural fruit juices)

6 x 10cm tartlet tins

Preheat the oven to 200°C/180°C fan/Gas mark 6.

Make 1 quantity of the sweet pastry on page 86, use it to line the tartlet tins, and refrigerate. Do not blind bake, as this step is not necessary for tartlets.

Put the coconut oil, spelt flour and coconut palm sugar in a bowl. Using your fingertips, rub the coconut oil into the flour and coconut palm sugar, until the mixture resembles large breadcrumbs. Add the oats, ground almonds, lemon zest and maple syrup. Combine with a spoon until everything is well mixed. It should look like wet sand.

Evenly divide the mixture between the 6 chilled tartlet cases. Slice the apricots into ½cm wedges and divide them between the tartlets. Scatter over a few redcurrants, if using, place the tartlets on a baking tray and bake for 45 minutes, until golden and set. Cover with foil if the top is browning too quickly. Remove and leave to cool.

Once the tartlets have cooled to room temperature, mix the apricot jam with 2 teaspoons of boiling water and use this to glaze the tartlets, using a pastry brush. Serve immediately with extra redcurrants if you wish.

fig and pistachio frangipane tart

A classic frangipane is the perfect base for any fresh seasonal fruit. Of course you could bake the fruit into the tart – but when they are in their first flushes of sunny seasonality, it seems a shame not to let them shine out in a totally unadulterated fashion, as I have done here. Feel free to use any other nut for the frangipane, and you can swap in another fruit for the topping – berries, fresh juicy nectarines – whatever you like.

1 quantity of sweet
shortcrust pastry
(see page 86)

frangipane

350g raw pistachio nuts
or almonds, plus extra
to decorate (optional)

250g extra virgin
coconut oil or
unsalted butter

250g coconut palm
sugar

2 tsp vanilla bean
paste or extract

zest of 1 unwaxed
lemon

pinch of sea salt

3 eggs, beaten

3 tbsp white spelt flour

to serve

10 figs, quartered
honey, to drizzle
yoghurt (Greek, soy
or coconut – optional)

Preheat the oven to 200°C/180°C fan/Gas mark 6.

Make the pastry case according to the method on page 86.

Roast the pistachios or almonds on a baking tray for 5–6 minutes, until they are a shade darker and aromatic. Leave to cool, then pulse in a food processor until they resemble large breadcrumbs. Take care not to grind the nuts to a powder. Move the mixture to a large bowl.

Add the coconut oil or butter, coconut palm sugar, vanilla, lemon zest and salt to the food processor. Blitz until light and fluffy. Add this mixture to the pistachios, together with the eggs and flour. Mix well until fully combined.

Tip the frangipane into the blind-baked tart shell and smooth out. Return it to the oven and bake for 35–40 minutes, until the tart has firmed up around the edges, but retains a little wobble towards the centre. Leave to cool, then turn the tart out of the tin on to a platter. Arrange the figs on the top, and drizzle over a little honey and a scattering of pistachio nuts. Serve in slices, with yoghurt if you like.

oat and cherry pie

serves 10–12

There's a little place called Jeannine's in Montecito, just outside Santa Barbara – and it endures in my mind as the most quintessentially all-American café and bakery one could imagine; the kind of place the Brady Bunch would have frequented after church on Sunday for some homespun nourishment. I ate an oat and cherry pie here that was so smotheringly good it assumed an almost unattainable deliciousness in my memory, and for years I never attempted to recreate it. Eventually I tried out a few different versions, and this is the result. Whether Jeannine would approve I don't know, but until I move to California this will have to do.

base

120g extra virgin coconut oil or unsalted butter, at room temperature

100g coconut palm sugar

1 tsp vanilla extract

90g white spelt flour

80g wholegrain spelt flour, or more white spelt flour

filling

80g coconut palm sugar

120g extra virgin coconut oil or unsalted butter, melted

1 tsp vanilla extract

2 eggs

80g white or wholegrain spelt flour

350g fresh cherries, halved and stoned

Preheat the oven to 200°C/180°C fan/Gas mark 6, and line the cake tin with greaseproof paper.

For the base, beat together the coconut oil or butter with the coconut palm sugar and vanilla extract, until the sugar has mostly dissolved and the mixture is light. Mix in the flours and thoroughly combine to form a dough. Press this into the base and sides of the lined tin, so you have an even crust with sides measuring about 2.5cm high. Cover and chill in the freezer for 10 minutes. Prick the base of the pastry with a fork, line it with baking parchment, fill it with baking beans and bake for 20 minutes. Remove the parchment and beans and bake for a further 5 minutes, until the tart shell is cooked through and biscuity.

While that is baking, make the filling. Beat together the coconut palm sugar, coconut oil or butter and vanilla extract until the sugar has mostly dissolved and the mixture is light. Mix in the eggs and flour, a bit at a time, until combined. Stir in the rest of the ingredients (apart from the jam) until thoroughly

70g jumbo oats

40g pumpkin seeds, plus
a few extra to scatter

40g sunflower seeds

¼ tsp ground cinnamon
(optional)

pinch of sea salt

5 tbsp cherry jam,
or other jam

to serve

yoghurt (Greek, soy
or coconut)

23cm round springform
cake tin

combined. Spread the cherry jam over the pastry base, top with
the filling, and scatter over a few pumpkin seeds. Place the tin on
a baking sheet and bake for 25–30 minutes, until the edges are
firm but the centre is still slightly unset. Remove and leave to cool
completely before serving – this is important, otherwise it will not
set properly.

chocolate hazelnut tart

serves 12–14

This combination of hazelnut and chocolate creates a delicious and healthy version of a Nutella tart. I love the flavour of coconut oil in place of butter in a frangipane, but of course you can swap in the same amount of unsalted butter if you prefer.

1 quantity of chocolate pastry (see page 87)

chocolate frangipane filling

275g skinned hazelnuts, plus extra to decorate (optional)

225g extra virgin coconut oil or unsalted butter

225g coconut palm sugar

2 tsp vanilla bean paste or extract

zest of 1 unwaxed lzmon

pinch of sea salt

3 eggs, beaten

3 tbsp white spelt flour

100g dark chocolate, minimum 70% cocoa solids

to serve

cocoa powder

sea salt

yoghurt (Greek or coconut, optional)

Preheat the oven to 200°C/180°C fan/Gas mark 6.

Make the chocolate pastry case according to the method on page 87.

Spread out the hazelnuts on a baking tray and bake for 5–6 minutes, until they are a shade darker. Leave to cool, then pulse in a food processor until they resemble large breadcrumbs. Take care not to grind them to a powder. Move the mixture to a large bowl.

Put the coconut oil or butter, coconut palm sugar, vanilla, lemon zest and salt in a food processor, and blitz until light and fluffy. Add this mixture to the hazelnuts, together with the eggs and flour. Stir to combine.

Melt the chocolate in a heatproof bowl set over a pan of simmering water. Add the melted chocolate to the frangipane and stir quickly until it all comes together into a homogenous mixture.

Add the frangipane to the blind-baked tart shell, and smooth it out. Bake for 35–40 minutes, until the tart has firmed up around the edges but retains a little wobble towards the centre. Remove from the oven and leave to cool, then turn the tart out of the tin on to a serving platter. Sift over a tablespoon or 2 of cocoa powder and sprinkle over a few sea salt crystals and hazelnuts. Serve in slices, with yoghurt if you like.

pear tarte Tatin

serves 4–6

The great thing about tarte Tatin is that it is supposed to look rustic and misshapen – in fact, the more uneven and random the shape and position of the pastry and pears, the better it looks. Traditionally it is made with cane sugar, but the coconut palm sugar and maple syrup make a seriously delicious and more deeply flavoured alternative.

1 quantity of sweet shortcrust pastry (see page 86)

4 firm Conference pears

1 tbsp lemon juice

50ml maple syrup

50g coconut palm sugar

50g flavourless extra virgin coconut oil or unsalted butter, or half of each

2 vanilla pods, split lengthways

¼ tsp ground cinnamon

pinch of sea salt

yoghurt (Greek, soy or coconut) or ice cream, to serve

20cm ovenproof pan

Make the sweet pastry according to the recipe on page 86, up to and including placing the raw pastry in the fridge to rest for 30 minutes.

Peel, core and quarter the pears lengthways. Toss them with the lemon juice and keep to one side.

Preheat the oven to 200°C/180°C fan/Gas mark 6.

Put the maple syrup, coconut palm sugar, coconut oil or butter, vanilla pods, cinnamon and salt into an ovenproof pan and set it over a medium heat. Cook for 4–5 minutes, until the sugar has dissolved and the mixture is syrupy. Add the pear quarters, curved side facing down, and cook for 10–15 minutes over a medium heat, shaking the pan from time to time to keep the pears from sticking, until they are tender and a deep golden brown.

While the pears are cooking, remove the pastry from the fridge and roll it out thinly. Cut out a disc that is roughly the size of the pan you are using. Any left over pastry can be used to make mini tarts. Position the pastry over the top of the pears and tuck the edges down around the side of the fruit, using the tip of a knife to help you tease it into place, so that it is a snug fit. Transfer the pan to the oven and bake for

35–40 minutes, until the pastry is golden and biscuity. Remove the pan from the oven and leave the tart to cool for 5 minutes. Loosen the edge with a knife, then in one swift movement, invert the tarte Tatin on to a large plate – taking care, as the liquid will still be very hot. Serve immediately, with yoghurt or ice cream.

berry pie

serves 8

There was a little café around the corner from a flat I lived in years ago in Brooklyn Heights, New York, which served the most stunning-looking 'all American' berry pies with incredibly decorative pastry. I had such high hopes, but sadly they turned out to be all show, as the fillings were overly sweet and gelatinous with no real fruit flavour. Years later I saw Christopher Kimball, the chef and presenter of America's Test Kitchen, explain that most commercial berry pies have masses of gelatine or flour added to them to ensure the juice from the berries sets, resulting in these tasteless fillings. One way to avoid this, he said, is to lower the quantity of tapioca or cornflour used, and add in a grated apple – it is high in pectin, which helps the filling to set naturally and doesn't mask the lovely flavour of the fresh fruit. I tried out a few different tarts this way and it works really well; the flavour of the fruit is vibrant and fresh, yet it holds together just enough to make it easy to slice. This should be made ahead of time, as it must cool to room temperature before being sliced.

pastry

355g white spelt flour, plus extra to dust

¾ tsp fine sea salt

160g extra virgin coconut oil or unsalted butter, chilled and cut into small pieces

2 tbsp maple syrup

filling

700g blueberries

cont.

For the pastry, put the flour and salt into the bowl of a food processor. Add the chilled coconut oil or butter and blitz until the mixture resembles fine breadcrumbs. Add the maple syrup and 2½–3 tablespoons of water and bring the dough together with your hands until it is in a smooth ball. If it is still crumbly, add a few drops of water at a time until it comes together into a smooth dough, being careful not to overdo it. Divide the dough in half, flatten it into discs, wrap it in cling film and refrigerate for 20 minutes, until well chilled but still pliable.

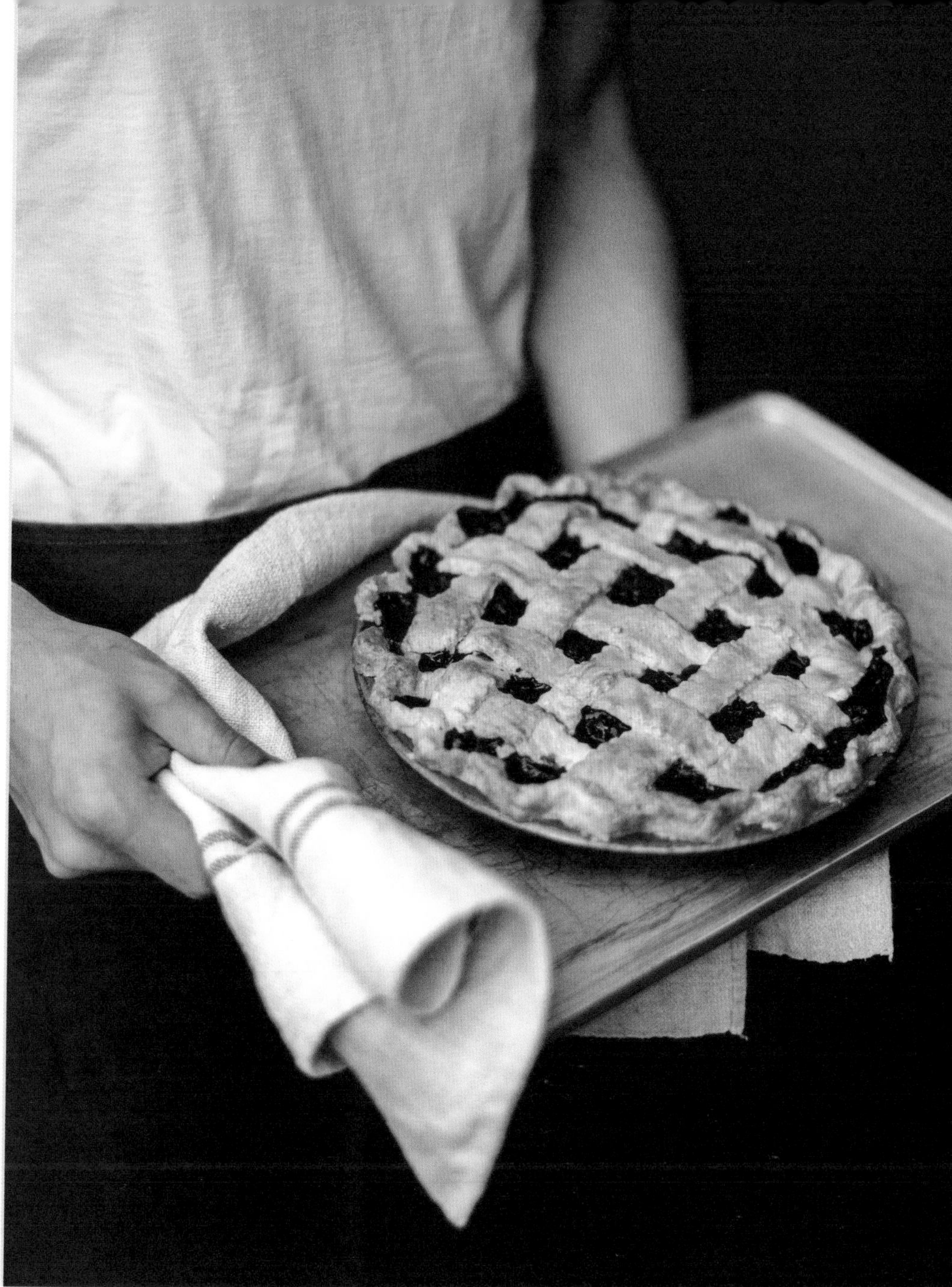

300g blackberries

160g coconut palm sugar, plus extra to sprinkle over

1 tsp vanilla paste

zest of 1 unwaxed lemon and 1 tbsp juice

2 tbsp tapioca flour or cornflour

pinch of sea salt

1 Granny Smith apple, peeled and coarsely grated

1 egg, beaten

pinch or 2 of coconut palm sugar

24cm American pie pan or fluted tart tin

For the filling, put half the blueberries and all the blackberries into a saucepan with the sugar and vanilla paste. Crush the berries with a potato masher and bring to the boil over a high heat, then reduce the heat to medium and simmer briskly for 20–25 minutes, until the sugar has dissolved and the mixture has reduced and thickened considerably. Remove the pan from the heat and stir in the remaining blueberries, lemon zest, lemon juice, tapioca flour or cornflour and salt. Wrap the grated apple in a clean tea towel and twist out as much liquid as possible. Stir the now dried apple into the mixture, and leave it to cool.

Preheat the oven to 200°C/180°C fan/Gas mark 6. Grease the pie pan or tart tin.

Remove 1 disc of pastry from the fridge. Roll it out between 2 sheets of floured cling film and line the base of the pan or tin, leaving about 2cm overhanging the edge. If you find the pastry too difficult to handle when rolling out, simply press the pastry directly into the tin, making sure the base and sides are smooth and even with no cracks. Cover and refrigerate. Roll out the second disc of pastry in the same way and either leave it whole, or cut it into strips so you can create a lattice.

Once the filling is cool, pour it into the chilled base, brush the edges of the bottom layer of pastry with some of the beaten egg, then position the top layer of pastry on top, or weave the strips of pastry on top to create a lattice. Fold the top and bottom edges of pastry underneath themselves on the ridge of the tin, then seal them together with your fingers or with a fork. If you have covered the pie with a single layer of pastry, cut 2 incisions in the centre with a sharp knife to allow steam to escape. Brush the pastry with the remaining beaten egg and sprinkle over a pinch or 2 of coconut palm sugar.

Bake the tart for 25 minutes, then turn the heat down to 180°C/160°C fan/Gas mark 4 and continue to bake for another 35–40 minutes, until the top is crisp and a rich golden brown colour. If it is browning too quickly, cover with a layer of foil. Remove from the oven and leave to cool completely in the tin, for at least a few hours, otherwise the filling will not be properly set.

plum and raspberry buckwheat crumble

serves 8

This plum, raspberry and buckwheat crumble is like a warm and familiar embrace – the ultimate in comfort puddings. The trick is to not make the crumble cloyingly sweet, which only masks the elegant sour notes of the plums and raspberries. The buckwheat flour is the perfect companion in this crumble; just the lightest of earthy notes to ground the sharper flavour of the fruit.

50g white spelt flour

30g buckwheat flour, or more spelt flour

60g extra virgin coconut oil or unsalted butter, chilled

70g rolled oats

190g coconut palm sugar

25g sunflower seeds

25g pumpkin seeds

pinch of sea salt

600g plums, stoned and cut into quarters

200g raspberries

zest of 1 unwaxed lemon

1 tsp vanilla extract

1½ tbsp cornflour

ice cream or yoghurt (Greek, soy or coconut), to serve

1 medium-sized pie dish

Preheat the oven to 200°C/180°C fan/Gas mark 6.

In a large bowl, combine the spelt and buckwheat flours. Rub in the coconut oil or butter until you have gravel-sized lumps. Add the oats, 60g of the coconut palm sugar, the sunflower and pumpkin seeds and a pinch of salt, and mix together. Set aside.

Put the quartered plums and the raspberries in a large bowl, and combine with the remaining 130g of sugar, the lemon zest, vanilla extract and cornflour. Transfer the mixture to the pie dish and top with the crumble – but don't press it down. Bake for 20–25 minutes, until golden brown. Remove from the oven and leave to cool for 5 minutes, then serve with ice cream or yoghurt.

chocolate, tahini and pecan rye cookies

**makes 20
large cookies**

I am of the 'crispy on the outside, slightly soft and chewy in the middle' band of cookie lovers. I know this can be a contentious area, so I won't try to convince you of my reasoning – whichever camp you fall into, these cookies are seriously good, not too sweet and with just enough rye, tahini and coconut oil to make them almost good for you. Almost.

150g white spelt flour

100g wholegrain
rye flour

½ tsp baking powder

130g extra virgin
coconut oil or
unsalted butter

40g tahini

250g coconut palm sugar

1 tsp sea salt, plus more
to scatter over

2 tsp vanilla extract

2 eggs

175g dark chocolate,
chopped into
small pieces

150g pecans, lightly
roasted at 180°C/160°C/
Gas mark 4 until a shade
darker, roughly chopped

Preheat the oven to 190°C/170°C fan/Gas mark 5 and line 3 baking sheets with baking parchment.

Put the flours and baking powder in a bowl, and stir to combine. Set aside.

Gently melt the coconut oil or butter in a saucepan over a low heat. Add the tahini, coconut palm sugar, salt and vanilla, and stir to combine until softened. Remove from the heat and transfer the mixture to a large mixing bowl. Allow to cool for a minute or 2, then add the eggs and whisk quickly, until everything comes together into a thick glossy mixture. Stir in the flour mixture, chocolate chips and chopped pecans until everything is just combined. Leave to cool for a few minutes.

Divide the mixture into 20 equal portions. If you want to be exact, you can weigh the entire dough and divide that weight by 20; it should be about 52g per cookie. This may seem a lot, but it works perfectly for large, chunky cookies. Roll each of the 20 pieces of dough into a ball and place them on the baking sheets with at least 6cm between them. Lightly flatten the balls and bake for 10–11 minutes, until the cookies have crispy edges and slightly soft centres.

Carefully transfer the cookies to a wire rack and leave to cool. Don't be tempted to cook the cookies for longer, even if they seem soft, as they will firm up considerably as they cool. Once completely cold, store in an airtight container for up to 1 week – but there is not the remotest possibility of them lasting that long.

coconut, tahini and cranberry macaroons

makes 14–16 macaroons

These are not at all like the dainty, pastel-coloured macaroons one scoffs when trying to feign an air of French sophistication. In fact, they are the opposite: more American in size and form, and not a bit elegant, but no less delicious. They are also far easier and quicker to make, which is never a bad thing.

110g tahini

45g dried cranberries

pinch of sea salt

zest and juice of ½ unwaxed lemon

100ml maple syrup

25g white spelt flour or rice flour

1 tsp bicarbonate of soda

220g desiccated coconut

80g dark chocolate, melted

Preheat the oven to 180°C/160°C fan/Gas mark 4, and line a baking sheet with greaseproof paper.

Put all the ingredients except the melted chocolate into a large bowl and mix together until thoroughly combined. The mixture is quite dry, but persevere until everything is mixed together.

Place 2 tablespoons of mixture into the palm of your hand and compress to form a ball. Lightly flatten into a disc and position on a baking sheet, leaving a 2cm gap in between each macaroon. Bake for 8 minutes, until lightly golden.

Remove from the oven and leave to cool completely to firm up. Dip the cooled macaroons into the melted chocolate and set aside in a cool spot until the chocolate has set. Keep in an airtight container in the fridge for up to 1 week.

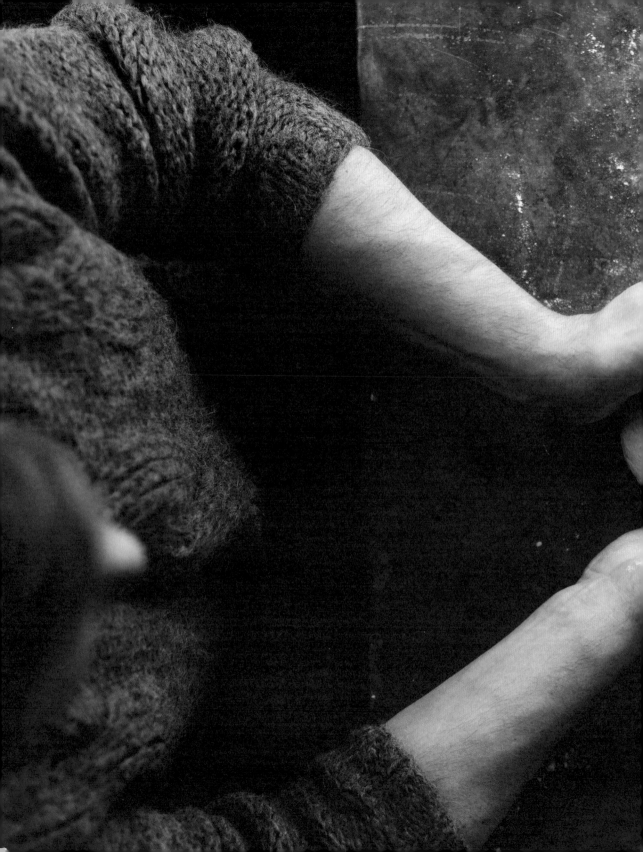

savoury baking

Baking is so much more than breads and cakes. These savoury tarts, frittatas, pizzas and whole baked vegetables are perfect for a casual get-together with friends or a weeknight dinner, and they are just as delicious the next day for a packed lunch. I tend to cook the tarts and pizzas when I have a little more time on my hands, usually on the weekend, whereas things like the whole baked cauliflower (page 130) or roast fennel, squash, chorizo and basil frittata (page 118) are ideal for a weeknight dinner.

pizzetta

makes about 10
small pizzetta,
or 5 large pizzas

There is a lot of ego surrounding the making of pizza
these days – 'secret' recipes and 'special' flour blends.
It's all nonsense, and a bit of a shame as it puts people
off making it at home. In fact, as long as your oven
can heat up to at least 240°C/220°C fan/Gas mark 9
and you have the right ingredients, you can make truly
delicious pizza yourself. Here I have used spelt and a
little rye flour, which make a really delicious dough,
but you could also use strong bread flour or '00' Italian
flour if you wish.

I use a baking stone at home, as the intense even
heat makes for a very authentic pizza base – slightly
charred, and crispy and chewy in all the right places.
A stone is a good investment if you think you will be
making pizza with any regularity, but if not, the base
of an upturned heavy baking tray is perfectly fine.

As for what ingredients should adorn your pizza, well
that is entirely up to you, so I have just provided a list
of topping suggestions and notes, from which you can
make your own. If I had my way, though, pineapple on
pizza would be outlawed!

dough

475g white spelt or
Italian 00 flour, plus
extra to dust

25g white rye flour,
or more spelt/00 flour

1 x 7g sachet of instant
yeast

2 tsp honey or
maple syrup

310ml warm water

20ml olive oil

10g fine sea salt

semolina, to dust

Sift the flours into a mixing bowl. Stir the yeast and
honey or maple syrup into the warm water to dissolve,
add to the flour with the olive oil and salt, and
combine until the mixture comes together into a ball.
Add a few more drops of water if necessary, but only
enough to bring it together.

Knead the dough for about 6–10 minutes, until it feels
springy, smooth and elastic. A stand mixer will do this
in about half the time. Dust with flour and place in

Tomato sauce, garlic and herb oils (see page 226), truffle oil, pesto

mozzarella, Parmesan, ricotta, Tallegio, Gorgonzola, feta, truffle shavings

onions, cherry tomatoes, blanched green vegetables like broccoli or kale, asparagus, waxy potatoes (boiled and thinly sliced), eggs, spinach, dried or fresh chilli, any fresh herbs, olives, sundried tomatoes, rocket, radicchio, fried mushrooms, grilled veg like peppers, aubergines, courgettes

anchovies, tuna, prawns, bacon, cured meats like speck, prosciutto, etc.

olive oil

herbs

a bowl covered with oiled cling film. Leave to rise for 1–1½ hours, or until it is at least doubled in size. The time will depend on how warm your kitchen is. You can also leave it to rise overnight in the fridge.

Preheat the oven to its hottest setting, or at least 240°C/220°C fan/Gas mark 9 and place your baking stone or upturned baking tray within it.

Once the dough has doubled in size, knead it once or twice and bring it into a ball. Divide the dough into 10 equal pieces to make individual pizzettas, or a few larger balls for bigger sharing pizzas. These can be wrapped in cling film at this point and frozen for use at a later date.

To cook the pizzetta, dust 1 of the balls with flour and gently stretch it out to a very thin round or oblong shape. A rolling pin is helpful for this. Don't worry about achieving perfectly uniform circles; in fact I much prefer the character of slightly misshapen pizzas.

Generously dust a pizza peel or a thin flat chopping board with the semolina, and lay the pizza base on top. Jiggle it around to make sure it is not sticking. Top with your choice of ingredients, transfer the pizza to the preheated baking stone or upturned baking tray and cook for 5–10 minutes, until crispy at the edges – the time will depend on the heat of your oven and whether you are using a baking stone.

Serve immediately, topped with a little drizzle of olive oil and any extra herbs you like. Continue to cook the rest of the pizzas as above.

sourdough pizza

To make sourdough pizza, simply follow the recipe for the spelt sourdough loaf on page 26, but use all white spelt flour. Prove the dough overnight as per the method, then divide it into equal balls, depending on the size of pizza you want. Shape and cook the pizzas following the method above.

roast fennel, squash, chorizo and basil frittata

serves 6–8

Fennel takes on a whole new world of flavour when roasted: gone are the brassier aniseed notes, and in their place comes an altogether more rounded and buttery deliciousness, sure to win over even the most ardent fennel-phobe. A simple baked frittata is an incredibly easy and satisfying way to put dinner on the table, and is ideal for anyone with an aversion to making pastry.

400g butternut squash, peeled, deseeded and cut into 2cm thick wedges

300g fennel, outer leaves removed, cut into 2cm thick wedges

3 tbsp olive oil, plus 1 tsp and extra to drizzle

1 red onion, thinly sliced

150g chorizo, skinned and sliced

250g spinach, washed

10–12 free range organic eggs – depending on the size of your pan

small bunch of basil

1 garlic clove, crushed

4 tbsp extra virgin olive oil

Mixed-leaf salad (optional), to serve

sea salt and pepper

24–26cm ovenproof pan or quiche dish

Preheat the oven to 200°C/180°C fan/Gas mark 6.

Toss the squash and fennel with 3 tablespoons of olive oil, and season well. Roast for 20–25 minutes, until golden and just tender.

10 minutes before the squash and fennel are cooked through, toss the red onion and chorizo in 1 teaspoon of olive oil, season with salt and pepper, and add to the tray. Roast for another 10 minutes, then remove and leave to one side.

Meanwhile, put the spinach in a large dry pan over a high heat. Turn the spinach as it wilts, then remove and drain in a sieve, pressing out any excess water. Season the spinach with a little salt and a drizzle of olive oil.

Crack the eggs into a bowl, whisk and season well. Put most of the squash, fennel, spinach, onion and chorizo into the ovenproof pan or quiche dish. Pour over the beaten egg and finish with the remaining fillings so that they stick out over the top of the egg.

Cook in the oven for about 35–45 minutes, until the frittata has souffléd up and the top is just firm to the touch. If it is still uncooked in the centre, cover with foil to prevent burning and cook until just firm.

While the frittata is cooking, chop the basil finely and combine with the garlic and the extra virgin olive oil, to create a loose basil oil.

Let the frittata cool a little, drizzle over the basil oil and serve immediately with a light mixed-leaf salad.

farinata with olives, red onion and rocket

**makes 2 farinata
(to serve 2)**

I have been making this chickpea flour pancake at least once or twice a week for many years. It is really quick to cook, but filling and full of strong Mediterranean flavours – grassy extra virgin olive oil and sweet red onion. You will find versions of this humble pancake all along the Cote d'Azur – I first discovered it in Nice, where it is known as socca, and it is slightly thinner than farinata. If you jump on the train and head on into Italy, all along the Ligurian Coast you will find this slightly spongier version. Whichever version you try, it is nearly always cooked on a very large cast-iron pan in a searingly hot wood-fired oven, then served very simply with some black pepper. While I have used olives, red onion and rocket here, you could easily swap these out for your favourite toppings; it is very adaptable.

200g chickpea flour,
also known as gram or
besan flour

320ml sparkling water

7 tbsp extra virgin olive
oil, plus extra to drizzle

2 handfuls of rocket

about 30 black and
green olives, stoned
and roughly chopped

1 red onion, finely
chopped

fine sea salt and
black pepper

24cm non-stick
ovenproof frying pan

Preheat the oven to 240°C/220°C fan/Gas mark 9.

Sift the chickpea flour and ½ teaspoon of salt into a large bowl. Slowly whisk in the sparkling water and 3 tablespoons of extra virgin olive oil, ensuring there are no lumps remaining.

Put 2 tablespoons of the olive oil into the frying pan and set it over a high heat. When the oil is very hot, almost smoking, pour in half the batter, swirling it around so it is evenly distributed. Leave on the high heat for exactly 30 seconds, then put it in the oven and cook for 4 minutes, or until it is set and the underside is crispy. Flip on to a large plate so the crispy underside is uppermost, and drizzle over 1½ tablespoons of extra virgin olive oil, as this helps both the flavour and texture of the farinata. Cook the second pancake in the same way with the remaining olive oil and batter.

To serve, season with a small pinch of salt and pepper. Divide the rocket, olives and red onion between the 2 pancakes, and serve immediately.

savoury spelt pastry

250g white or wholegrain spelt flour, plus extra to dust

½ tsp fine sea salt

120g flavourless extra virgin coconut oil or unsalted butter, chilled and cut into small pieces

Preheat the oven to 200°C/180°C fan/Gas mark 6.

Put the flour and salt into the bowl of a food processor. Add the chilled coconut oil or butter and blitz until it resembles fine breadcrumbs. Add 2½–3 tablespoons of water and bring the dough together with your hands until it is in a smooth ball. If it is still crumbly, add in a few drops of water at a time, being careful not to overdo it. Flatten the dough out into a disc, wrap it in cling film and refrigerate for 20–30 minutes, until chilled but still pliable.

Roll out the pastry between two sheets of floured cling film and line the tart tin called for in the recipe. If you find the pastry too difficult to handle, simply press the pastry directly into the tin, making sure the base and sides are smooth and even with no cracks. Cover and chill for 15 minutes, or 5 minutes in the freezer. Prick the base of the pastry all over with a fork, line with baking parchment, fill with baking beans, and bake for 20 minutes. Remove the parchment and beans and bake for a further 5 minutes, until the tart shell is dry and biscuity.

spelt and rye pastry

50g rye flour

Follow the savoury spelt pastry recipe above with the same ingredients, but reduce the spelt flour to 200g and add 50g of rye flour.

gluten-free savoury pastry

250g gluten-free flour mix

½ tsp fine sea salt

¼ tsp xanthan gum

120g flavourless coconut oil or unsalted butter, chilled and cut into small pieces

Follow the same method as the savoury spelt pastry, adding the xanthan gum to the gluten-free flour and salt mixture.

caramelised onion, sweet potato and rye tart

serves 8–10

This is perfect for a casual dinner party, as all the work is done in advance. I usually have everything ready beforehand, as it takes a bit of time to prepare, then fire it into the oven just as our friends arrive. The smell of it baking is as much a part of the enjoyment as the eating of it.

1 quantity of spelt and rye pastry (see page 123)

5 tbsp olive oil

5 onions, halved and thinly sliced

2 tbsp chopped fresh thyme leaves

2 medium sweet potatoes, about 450g, halved and cut into 2cm wedges

3 eggs, beaten

200ml coconut milk or single cream

3 garlic cloves, crushed

1 tsp cumin seeds

small bunch of basil, chopped

3 tbsp extra virgin olive oil

sea salt and pepper

24cm round or 35cm x 12cm rectangular tart tin

Preheat the oven to 200°C/180°C fan/Gas mark 6.

Heat 4 tablespoons of the olive oil in a non-stick frying pan over a low–medium heat. Add the onions and most of the thyme, and season with ½ teaspoon of sea salt and a grind of pepper. Cook over a gentle heat for 30–40 minutes, stirring occasionally, until golden and lightly caramelised. Take care not to burn the onions.

While the onions are cooking, make the spelt and rye tart shell according to the recipe on page 123.

Meanwhile, toss the sweet potato wedges in the remaining 1 tablespoon of olive oil, season with salt and pepper and bake for 20 minutes, until just softened and golden. They will finish cooking with the tart later.

Whisk together the eggs, coconut milk or cream, two-thirds of the crushed garlic, the cumin seeds and most of the basil, and season well with salt and pepper. Pour into the blind-baked pastry shell, top with the caramelised onions and pile over the sweet potato wedges. Cover completely with foil and bake for 25 minutes. Remove the foil and bake for a further 10–15 minutes, until golden and set.

While the tart is in the oven, combine the remaining thyme, basil, crushed garlic, a pinch of sea salt and the extra virgin olive oil. Drizzle over the tart when it is baked, and serve immediately.

thyme and tomato tarte Tatin

serves 4–6

Although tarte Tatin is better known for its sweet versions, it is equally delicious in a more savoury guise. Make sure to use vibrant red, ripe tomatoes, as the flavour will be greatly improved.

1 quantity of
savoury spelt pastry
(see page 123)

500g ripe baby plum
tomatoes

1 tbsp extra virgin
olive oil

2 tsp good-quality
aged balsamic vinegar

5 thyme sprigs

2 garlic cloves, crushed

2 tbsp basil pesto

sea salt and pepper

20cm ovenproof pan

Make the pastry according to the recipe on page 123, up to and including placing the raw pastry in the fridge to rest for 30 minutes.

Preheat the oven to 200°C/180°C fan/Gas mark 6.

In a bowl, toss the tomatoes together with the extra virgin olive oil and balsamic vinegar, and season. Place 2 of the thyme sprigs on the base of the ovenproof pan and pour over the tomatoes and dressing. Roast in the oven for 20–25 minutes until the tomatoes have burst open. Remove the pan, pour off as much of the juices as possible into a bowl and keep to use as a salad dressing or to drizzle over the tart once it is cooked. Redistribute the tomatoes in the pan.

Remove the pastry from the fridge and roll it out thinly. Cut out a disc that is roughly the size of the pan you are using. Combine the crushed garlic and pesto and spread it over the centre of the pastry. Position the pastry, pesto side down, over the top of the tomatoes and tuck the edges down around the side, using the tip of a knife to help you tease it into place around the tomatoes.

Transfer to the oven and bake for 40–45 minutes, until the pastry is golden and biscuity. Remove from the oven and leave to cool for 5 minutes. In one swift movement, invert the tarte Tatin onto a large plate – taking care, as the liquid will still be very hot. Top with the remaining thyme, and a drizzle of the reserved juices. Serve immediately.

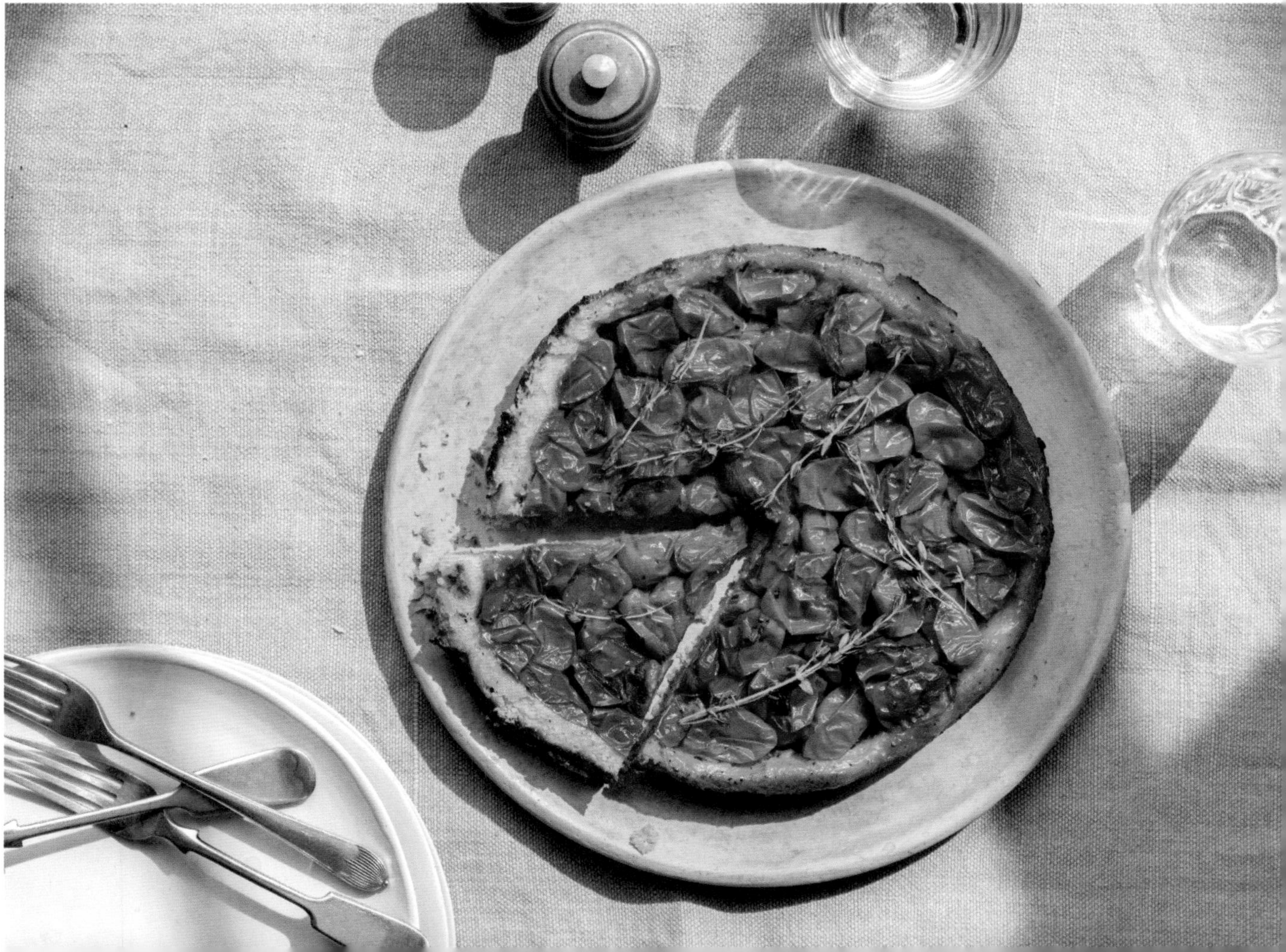

red onion, girolles and pine nut tart

serves 8

The wedges of soft red onion look so beautiful and pack in a lot of deep, subtly sweet flavour that works really well with the girolles. You could easily swap the girolles for another mushroom if you prefer.

1 quantity of
savoury spelt pastry
(see page 123)

3 red onions, halved and
cut into 2cm wedges

3 tbsp olive oil

250g girolles or
chestnut mushrooms,
sliced

4 eggs

100ml coconut cream
or double cream

2 garlic cloves, crushed

1 tsp sweet smoked
paprika

small bunch of parsley,
chopped

2 tbsp pine nuts,
roasted to garnish

sea salt and pepper

24cm round tart tin

Preheat the oven to 200°C/180°C fan/Gas mark 6 and grease the tart tin.

Toss the red onion wedges with 2 tablespoons of olive oil on a baking tray, and roast for 25–30 minutes in the oven, until slightly charred and softened.

Meanwhile, make the savoury spelt tart shell according to the recipe on page 123.

Add the remaining tablespoon of oil to a pan set over a high heat. Once it is hot, add the mushrooms and fry for 3 minutes, until golden. Season with salt and pepper and set to one side.

Whisk together the eggs, cream, garlic, smoked paprika and most of the parsley, and season well with salt and pepper. Pour the mixture into the blind-baked pastry shell, top with the red onions and mushrooms and bake for 30–35 minutes, until golden and set. Remove and leave to cool a little. Serve with the roasted pine nuts and remaining parsley scattered over the top.

whole baked cauliflower
with cumin tahini

**serves 2 as a main
or 4 as a side**

My wife and I often find ourselves in Paris for work, and when we have a bit of time off we try out some of the wonderful restaurants, and gorge ourselves on the incredibly fresh produce at the markets. One of our favourite spots is a buzzing little Israeli restaurant in le Marais called Miznon, an outpost of the original in Tel Aviv. They mainly sell stuffed pitta sandwiches, but the whole baked cauliflower created by the head chef, Eyal Shani, is almost iconic, and for good reason. They have a wood-fired oven that gives it an extra level of charred flavour from the ferocious heat, but you can create something at home that is every bit as delicious and satisfying; the key is letting it get properly charred, almost burnt in places.

cumin tahini

1 garlic clove, crushed

1 tsp red wine vinegar

1 tsp cumin seeds,
toasted

3 tbsp tahini

3 tbsp extra virgin olive
oil, plus extra to drizzle

small handful of parsley,
finely chopped

50ml water

pinch of sea salt

cauliflower

1 small cauliflower,
leaves still attached

1 tbsp olive oil,
for baking

sea salt

For the cumin tahini, put all the ingredients (leaving some parsley aside) into a bowl together and whisk vigorously until thoroughly combined. It should be the consistency of pouring cream. Taste and adjust the seasoning if necessary.

Preheat the oven to 240°C/220°C fan/Gas mark 9. Trim the base of the cauliflower so that it sits flat on a surface, but making sure that the leaves remain intact. Put the whole cauliflower and 1 tablespoon of salt into a large pot, and cover with water. Bring to the boil, then reduce the heat and simmer for 12–16 minutes, turning the cauliflower halfway through, until a sharp knife glides into the root end without too much resistance. Drain the cauliflower thoroughly, then return it to the hot pot (off the heat) to dry out for about 5–10 minutes.

Pour 1 tablespoon of olive oil into the palm of your hand and, with both hands, massage the oil all over the cauliflower head and leaves. Season well with salt, transfer to a baking tray and bake for 20–25 minutes, until golden and charred in places.

Remove from the oven, leave to cool for 5 minutes, then drizzle over a little extra virgin olive oil and serve immediately with the tahini sauce and the remaining parsley scattered over the top.

balsamic baked aubergines, mushrooms and farro

Slowly baking the aubergine and mushrooms with aged balsamic vinegar gives the vegetables a wonderfully deep, almost meaty, flavour. This dish is easily worthy of being the main event, but also works well as a side. Farro is an ancient grain with a delicious, slightly nutty flavour and a chewy consistency that is really satisfying. Do not confuse it with spelt, which has a much harder shell and takes far longer to cook. Alternatively, you can also use pearl barley, bulgur wheat or short-grain brown rice.

500g mixed mushrooms, such as portobello, shiitake, oyster or girolle, roughly chopped into 2cm thick slices

3 medium aubergines, cut into 1.5cm thick discs

5 garlic cloves, halved

5 tbsp good-quality aged balsamic vinegar, plus extra to serve

2 tbsp olive oil

200g farro, barley, short-grain brown rice or couscous

2 tbsp extra virgin olive oil

2 tsp soy sauce

small bunch of mint leaves, chopped

small bunch of flat-leaf parsley leaves, chopped

1 tbsp flaked almonds, roasted

sea salt and pepper

Preheat the oven to 200°C/180°C fan/Gas mark 6.

Put the sliced mushrooms into a large bowl with the aubergine discs and the garlic, combine with 4 tablespoons of the balsamic vinegar and the olive oil, and season well with salt and pepper, making sure everything is well coated. Spread the vegetables out on 2 baking sheets, making sure they are not all crowded together, otherwise they will steam and become soggy. Bake for 20–25 minutes, until deeply golden and tender.

Meanwhile, add the farro to a pot, cover with cold water and season well with salt. Bring to the boil, reduce the heat and simmer for 25–30 minutes, until tender but still chewy. (If using packets of 'quick-cook' farro, follow the packet instructions.) Drain well and, while still hot, season with the 2 tablespoons of extra virgin olive oil, soy sauce, the remaining tablespoon of balsamic vinegar and most of the herbs. Taste and adjust the seasoning if necessary.

Layer the vegetables and farro on a plate and sprinkle over the remaining herbs and the flaked almonds. Drizzle with a little more balsamic vinegar and serve immediately.

baked leeks, almonds and aioli

serves 4, as a side

This is a delicious and straightforward dish, ideal as a starter or side. If you don't want to make your own aioli (although I would encourage you to try, as there is nothing like it when freshly made), you can buy good-quality mayonnaise and add some crushed garlic and a little lemon juice.

6 leeks

2 tbsp olive oil, extra for toasting

50g almonds, skin on

1 tbsp chopped flat-leaf parsley

sea salt and pepper

aioli

1 egg yolk

1 tbsp lemon juice

1 garlic clove, crushed

75ml extra virgin olive oil

50ml olive or sunflower oil

Preheat the oven to 200°C/180°C fan/Gas mark 6, and bring a large pot of salted water to the boil.

Trim the leeks, but make sure you don't take too much off the top, or they will fall apart when sliced. Cut the leeks in half lengthways and rinse under running water to remove any soil. Add the leeks to the boiling water and cook for 3–4 minutes, until tender. Remove them from the water and drain well. Put the drained leeks in a roasting tray, drizzle over the olive oil, season and bake for 12–15 minutes, until slightly charred and crispy on the outside.

Meanwhile, roast the almonds in the oven for 6 minutes, until they are a shade darker and aromatic. Remove from the heat and leave to cool.

For the aioli, put the egg yolk, lemon juice, garlic and a good pinch of salt into the bowl of a food processor. While the motor is running, slowly drizzle in the olive (or sunflower) oil, taking care not to add it in too quickly, otherwise it will not emulsify with the egg yolk. Once incorporated, taste and adjust the seasoning with more salt and lemon juice if necessary. Transfer to a bowl and chill until ready to use.

Plate up the leeks, slice the toasted almonds into slivers, and scatter them over the leeks together with the parsley. Dollop over some aioli, and serve the rest on the side.

baked sweet potato and beetroot with roasted freekeh and salmoriglio

serves 4

Freekeh is dried young wheat, which is harvested while the grains are still soft and green, then roasted, giving it a lovely earthy and slightly smoky flavour. It is popular in the Middle East and North Africa but is now widely available the world over, and works as a great alternative to bulgur and couscous, although these grains would be delicious here too.

3 medium sweet potatoes, cut into 3cm wedges

4 beetroots, cut into 2cm wedges

3 tbsp olive oil, and 1 tsp for frying the pumpkin seeds

200g freekeh (quinoa, wild rice or any other grain can also be used here, cooked according to packet instructions)

3 tbsp thyme and rosemary salmoriglio (see page 215)

½ preserved lemon (see page 210, or shop bought), or zest of 1 unwaxed lemon

2 tbsp pumpkin seeds

sea salt and pepper

Preheat the oven to 200°C/180°C fan/Gas mark 6.

Toss the sweet potato and beetroot wedges in 2 tablespoons of the olive oil, and season well. Roast for 25–30 minutes, until they are golden and a sharp knife glides into the centre.

Meanwhile, put the freekeh into a saucepan and cover with water, then add 1 teaspoon salt and the remaining 1 tablespoon olive oil and bring to the boil. Reduce the heat to medium–low and simmer for 15 minutes, until tender. Drain and, while still hot, combine with half of the thyme and rosemary salmoriglio.

Cut the preserved lemon into wedges; remove the flesh so that only the skin remains, then slice into very thin strips. Stir into the freekeh.

Put the pumpkin seeds in a pan with 1 teaspoon oil and set over a high heat. Fry for 1–2 minutes, until crispy.

Plate up the sweet potato and beetroot with the freekeh. Drizzle over the remaining salmoriglio and scatter over the pumpkin seeds. Serve immediately.

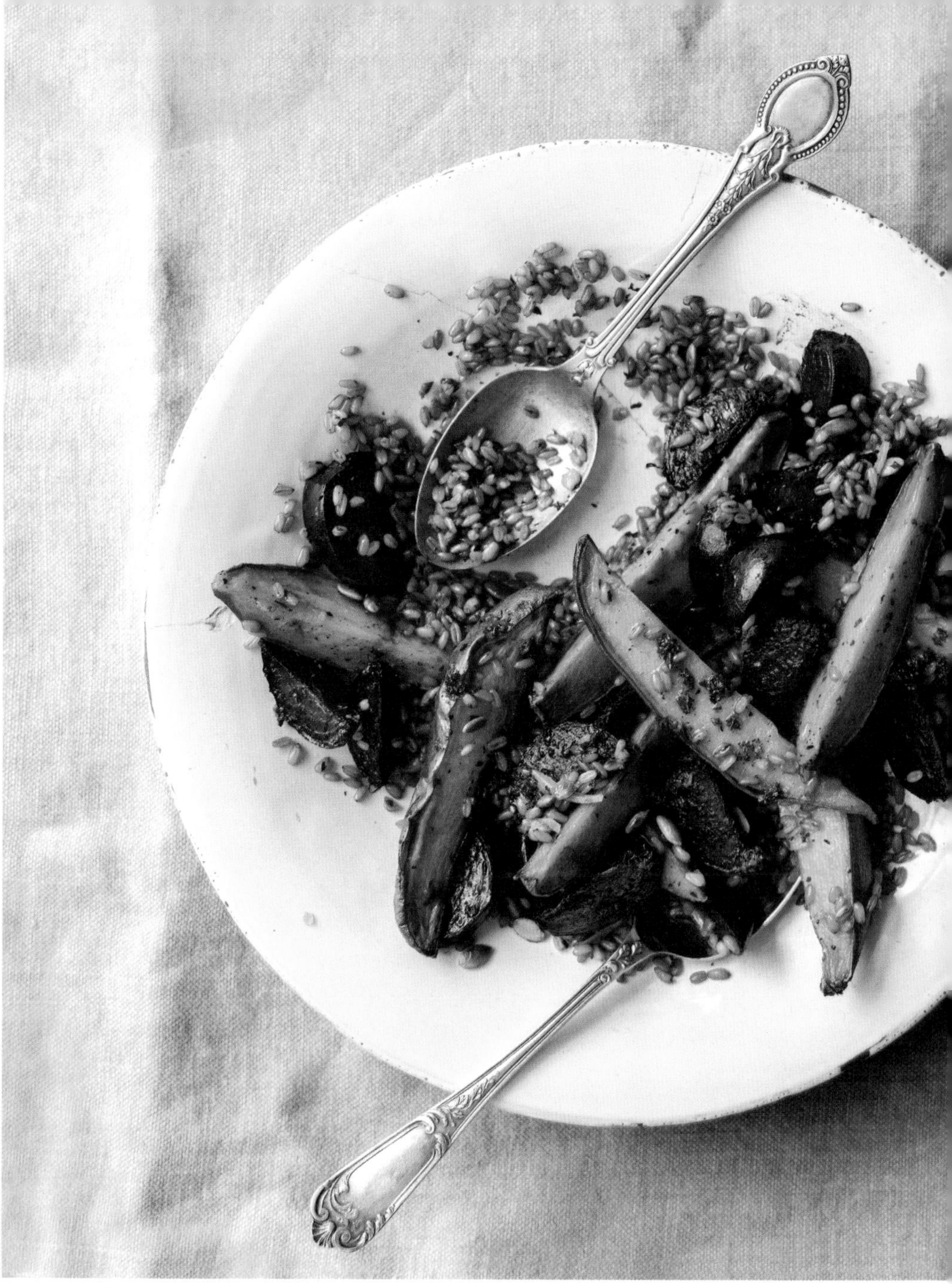

roasted carrots with kamut, thyme, hazelnuts and garlic yoghurt

serves 6

This is a seasonal combination of carrots, hazelnuts and grains. I have used kamut here, but spelt, barley, rye or farro all work well – and you can buy them in ready-to-eat pouches for ease. Rainbow carrots, vibrant with all their psychedelic colours, are a lovely addition to this dish if you come across them, but regular carrots are just as delicious.

50g blanched hazelnuts

1kg carrots – rainbow-coloured carrots are beautiful if you can find them

2 tbsp olive oil, plus extra for seasoning

handful of thyme sprigs, leaves picked, plus extra to serve

2 tsp cumin seeds

zest of 1 unwaxed lemon

250g ready-to-eat kamut, or another grain like spelt, barley, rye, etc.

sea salt and pepper

garlic yoghurt (see page 228)

Preheat the oven to 200°C/180°C fan/Gas mark 6.

Spread the hazelnuts out on a baking tray and roast for 4–5 minutes, until they are a shade darker and aromatic. Remove the nuts from the oven and leave to cool, then roughly chop.

Meanwhile, scrub the carrots, but don't peel them. Halve and quarter any large carrots lengthways, so that everything is roughly the same size. Put the carrots into a roasting tray and toss with 2 tablespoons of olive oil, the thyme leaves, cumin seeds and lemon zest, and season generously with salt and pepper. Roast for 25–30 minutes, until the carrots are golden and a sharp knife glides into the thickest part with little resistance.

Heat the ready-to-eat kamut, or whatever grain you are using, according to the packet instructions. Season to taste with olive oil, salt and pepper.

Layer the kamut and carrots on a platter with the remaining thyme, hazelnuts and yoghurt scattered over the top, or on the side in a small bowl to dip into.

make a meal with it

I think it is a testament to the great appeal of good-quality bread that so many dishes have been dreamt up over the years to make use of every last scrap of it, regardless of how many days old it might be. If you do not have any home-made bread you can of course use shop-bought bread, but I would encourage you to seek out real bread or sourdough from your local bakery.

Istanbul scrambled egg sourdough sandwich with feta and chorizo

serves 2

For my thirtieth birthday my wife surprised me with a trip to Istanbul, a city I had longed to visit for many years. It was over New Year, so the weather was truly awful! Despite the adverse conditions, or perhaps because of them, we had one of our most memorable trips to date. We spent the majority of each day running through the streets, in a bid to escape the driving rain, ducking in to cafés, restaurants and heaving market stalls as we went, with the excuse that we would need to stay a while to dry off! This was our last breakfast in Istanbul, and we have eaten it with fond memories ever since. Traditionally it is served with a Turkish spiced sausage called sucuk (aka sujuk), but chorizo is a good alternative. This is really good served with the chilli tomato jam on page 208.

2 tbsp olive oil

1 onion, finely chopped

1 tsp cumin seeds

2 garlic cloves, crushed

4 eggs, beaten

handful of parsley, finely chopped

80g feta, crumbled

2 small chorizo or sucuk sausages, halved lengthways

4 thin slices of spelt sourdough bread (see page 26, or shop bought)

extra virgin olive oil, to drizzle

Heat the olive oil in a large frying pan over a medium heat. Add the onion and sweat it down for 10 minutes, until translucent. Add the cumin and garlic and cook for another 2 minutes. Add the eggs and most of the parsley, and season well with salt and pepper. Turn the heat down low, stirring from time to time for about 4 minutes, or until the eggs are barely cooked and are still smooth and silky. Stir through the feta and leave to one side.

In a separate frying pan, fry the sausages over a high heat for 2 minutes on each side. Toast the bread slices briefly, just to warm them through; you don't want them crunchy at all.

chilli tomato jam to serve
(optional)

sea salt and back pepper

Drizzle a small amount of the extra virgin olive oil over the bread, top two slices with the scrambled egg and sausage, and sprinkle over the remaining parsley. Place the remaining 2 slices of bread on top, and serve with chilli tomato jam (see page 208) on the side, if you like.

kimchi, egg and avocado
on sourdough

serves 2

This is one of the dishes I make when I am trying to convince a sceptic that kimchi is one of the best ingredients in the world. The frying mellows out the sharper, more acidic notes, while adding in a slightly charred caramelised flavour that is sure to win over the most ardent kimchi-phobe. It always works. This dish can be eaten at any time of day. It has all the components of a sublime weekend breakfast or brunch, but is just as delicious at dinnertime.

2 tbsp olive oil, for frying

200g kimchi, chopped into bite-size pieces (see cabbage and kale kimchi, page 246, or shop bought)

1 tsp honey

½ tsp roasted sesame seed oil

2 eggs

2 large slices of spelt sourdough bread (see page 26, or shop bought)

1 small garlic clove, peeled

extra virgin olive oil, to drizzle

1 avocado, stoned and sliced

80g feta, broken into chunks

sea salt and pepper

Heat 1 tablespoon of the oil in a large frying pan over a high heat. When very hot, add the kimchi and fry for 3–4 minutes, stirring from time to time, until it starts to caramelise. Turn down the heat a little, add the honey and sesame seed oil and fry for another minute. Remove from the heat and leave to one side.

Heat the remaining tablespoon of oil in another frying pan over a high heat. When hot put in the eggs and fry for 3–4 minutes, until the egg whites are crispy around the edges and the egg yolks are still a little runny.

Toast the sourdough, then scrape the garlic over the top of each piece of toast, rubbing it into the surface. Season with a small pinch of salt and drizzle over some extra virgin olive oil.

Spoon the kimchi over the toast, and top with the avocado, fried egg and feta. Season with a little pepper and serve immediately.

bruschetta three ways

serves 6

Really this could be bruschetta one hundred and twenty-three ways – there are near-infinite topping possibilities – but these are three of my favourites. Of course traditionally, bruschetta is nothing more than good-quality stale bread charred over a grill, with grassy extra virgin olive oil, ripe tomatoes and young garlic . . . so I will admit I have got somewhat carried away with these suggestions. If you are a traditionalist, by all means keep it simple – it is just as magical. One thing to bear in mind is that the bread shares equal billing with whatever sits on top of it, so it must be thickly cut (at least 2cm) – little slivers won't do at all. There is enough going on here to make for a delicious, if casual, lunch, or it works really well as a starter. The toppings can also go into sandwiches or salads, and also make a delicious pasta sauce.

2 tbsp pine nuts

100ml olive oil

3 aubergines (about 800g) chopped into 2cm chunks

1 onion, roughly chopped

4 celery sticks, tough outer skin peeled and finely chopped

500g cherry tomatoes, halved

3 garlic cloves, crushed

1 tbsp coconut palm sugar or maple syrup

3 tbsp capers, rinsed and drained

80g black olives, Kalamata or similar, pitted and chopped

2 tbsp red wine vinegar

3 tbsp raisins

small handful of flat-leaf parsley, roughly chopped

small handful of basil, roughly chopped

sea salt and pepper

labneh (see page 216) or yoghurt (Greek, soy or coconut), to serve

1: aubergine caponata and labneh

Preheat the oven to 200°C/180°C fan/Gas mark 6.

Spread the pine nuts out on a baking tray and roast for 4 minutes, until golden. Set aside. Heat the oil in a large pot or pan with a lid, over a medium heat. Add the aubergine, season well and fry for about 10 minutes, until softened. Place the aubergine in a bowl. Add the onion and celery to the pan and sweat down for 10 minutes, until translucent and soft. Add the tomatoes, garlic, sugar, capers, olives, vinegar and raisins and fry over a low–medium heat for half an hour, until everything has softened and come together. Stir in the cooked aubergine, the herbs and the pine nuts. Taste and adjust the seasoning if necessary.

Serve warm piled on to toast with a dollop of labneh or yoghurt.

2: smashed chickpeas and avocado

2 tsp cumin seeds

1 x 400g tin of chickpeas, rinsed and drained

2 garlic cloves, crushed

zest of 1 lemon

3 tbsp extra virgin olive oil

small handful of parsley, shopped

1 avocado, peeled, stoned and cut into chunks

½ tsp dried chilli flakes, to serve

sea salt and pepper

Put the cumin seeds in a dry frying pan over a medium heat, and cook for a couple of minutes until they are a shade darker and aromatic. Watch carefully, as they burn easily. Bash them up a bit with a pestle and mortar to release the flavour, but leave a bit of texture. Put them back into the same pan, together with the chickpeas, garlic, lemon zest and olive oil, and set over a low heat. Lightly smash up half the chickpeas with a fork or potato masher, season to taste, and combine until the mixture is warmed through. Place in a bowl and stir through the parsley and avocado. Serve with the dried chilli flakes sprinkled over the top.

3: pea and mint purée

3 tbsp extra virgin olive oil

1 onion, finely chopped

400g peas

1 garlic clove

small handful of mint leaves

zest of 1 lemon

sea salt and pepper

Place a frying pan over a medium heat with 1 tablespoon of olive oil, add the onion and sauté for 10 minutes, until soft and translucent. Keep to one side.

Cook the peas in a pan of boiling, salted water for 3–4 minutes. Drain, and put them in a food processor with the onion, garlic, mint, lemon zest, remaining olive oil and ¾ teaspoon of sea salt. Pulse a few times on and off until combined but still retaining some texture. Taste and adjust the seasoning if necessary. Slather the pureé on to the bruschetta and sprinkle over some pepper.

the bruschetta

to serve

spelt sourdough bread slices (see page 26) – ideally they should be a little stale

1–2 garlic cloves

extra virgin olive oil

Toast the bread on a grill or in the toaster. Scrape the garlic over the crunchy exterior of the bread, drizzle over just a little olive oil and a tiny pinch of salt. Spoon on the toppings and arrange on a large serving dish.

Turkish mackerel sourdough sandwich

serves 2

On the Karakoy waterfront in Istanbul, stretching out along the Galata Bridge, you will find throngs of people queuing for balik ekmek, or 'fish bread' – a very simple, but hearty and delicious sandwich of grilled fish and salad. I have used sourdough here, but it is also delicious stuffed into pitta bread (see page 60) or a spelt wrap (see page 62).

3 tbsp cumin yoghurt (see page 228)

1 baby gem lettuce, roughly chopped

½ red onion, sliced

small handful of parsley leaves

2 tomatoes, deseeded and chopped

1 tsp chilli flakes

1 tbsp extra virgin olive oil

2 tsp red wine vinegar

2 tsp olive oil

2 mackerel fillets

1 unwaxed lemon, quartered

4 slices of spelt sourdough bread (see page 26, or shop bought)

2 tbsp harissa (see page 214 or shop bought, optional)

sea salt and pepper

Make the cumin yoghurt following the recipe on page 228.

For the salad, combine the lettuce, red onion, parsley, tomatoes, chilli flakes, extra virgin olive oil and vinegar. Set to one side.

Heat the olive oil in a pan over a medium–high heat. Season the mackerel generously on both sides with a good pinch of salt and pepper. When the oil is hot add in the mackerel fillets, skin side down. Fry for 2 minutes on 1 side, then flip over and fry for another 2 minutes, depending on the thickness of the fish. Remove the fish, brush the cut side of the lemon quarters with olive oil, place them cut side down and fry on a high heat until moderately charred.

Meanwhile, toast the sourdough, divide the salad between 2 slices of bread, top with the mackerel, cumin yoghurt and harissa and place the remaining sourdough on top.

make a meal with it

gazpacho

serves 4

1kg very ripe tomatoes, roughly chopped

3 garlic cloves

½ red onion, finely chopped or grated

120g cucumber

150g roast red pepper from a jar, or raw red pepper, deseeded

125g slightly stale spelt sourdough bread (see page 26, or shop bought), crusts removed

2 tbsp red wine vinegar

3 tbsp extra virgin olive oil, plus extra to serve

10 basil leaves, plus extra to serve

1½ tsp sea salt

¼ tsp freshly ground black pepper

4 heritage multi-coloured tomatoes, to serve (optional)

As a kid, a good chunk of my summer holidays were spent with my family in Vitoria in the north of Spain, partly because my dad loves camping and was insistent on us all discovering every back road Spain had to offer, and also because we are friends with a big Spanish family from the area. As a result I have strong memories associated with gazpacho: how I loathed it as a child – vivid and detailed recollections of the cool, shuttered Spanish kitchens and Formica tables where I tried to avoid eating it; and later on, how I came to adore it – my palate finally coming to terms with all those bright acidic flavours bouncing around the place. I don't recommend eating gazpacho unless it's a hot day; I just find the flavours and the experience of eating it are marred by cooler temperatures. This soup can be made a day in advance, but bear in mind that the flavour of the red wine vinegar intensifies, so it is advisable to add it in to taste the following day, when you are ready to serve it.

Place all the ingredients, apart from the heritage tomatoes, into an upright blender and blitz for up to 5 minutes depending on how powerful your blender is, until the soup is completely smooth. Taste and adjust the seasoning with a little more vinegar and salt if necessary. Refrigerate the gazpacho for at least 2 hours, or until very well chilled.

When ready to serve, taste it again to check for a good balance of flavours, as the flavours are dulled when chilled. Divide the soup between bowls, slice up the heritage tomatoes and position them on top, with a little drizzle of extra virgin olive oil, some black pepper and a few torn basil leaves. If it is a scorcher of a day, throw in a few ice cubes.

pan con tomate

This is not really a recipe as such, but it's so delicious in its simplicity it is worth including. Pan con tomate is an extremely popular snack and accompaniment to all sorts of tapas, originally in the regions of Catalunya and Valencia in Spain, but these days all over the country as well. As a child we had Spanish au pairs who would make it at least once a day – on its own for breakfast, or topped with tortilla or jamón for lunch or dinner. I never quite understood why they only used the pulp of the tomato, and not the skin – I did query them on the matter many times, but it wasn't really open for discussion. Now of course I can't eat it any other way, and I appreciate that it is all about the juice seeping down into the bread. I do keep the tomato skins for use in a salad, though!

2 slices of spelt
sourdough bread
(see page 26, or
shop bought)

1 garlic clove, peeled

2 large, very ripe and
juicy tomatoes

2 tsp extra virgin
olive oil

sea salt

Lightly toast or grill the bread – it should not take on too much colour.

Scrape the garlic over the top of each piece of toast, rubbing it into the surface, or crush it and spread it over the surface with a knife.

Slice the tomatoes in half and squeeze all of the juice and pulp directly on to the bread, saturating the surface. Drizzle a teaspoon of the oil over each slice and season with salt.

Leave it to soak up the juices for a minute or 2. Serve immediately.

spanish bread
and almond soup

serves 4–6

Known as ajo blanco, this soup hails from Andalucia, the hot and arid part of southern Spain, so it's no surprise that it is served chilled. I blanch the almonds myself as I find the flavour is greatly improved, but if you are short on time you can of course buy ready blanched almonds.

200g whole almonds, skin on

50g spelt sourdough bread (see page 26, or shop bought), crusts removed

2 garlic cloves

250ml extra virgin olive oil, plus extra to serve

430ml ice-cold water

1½ tbsp sherry vinegar

small handful of grapes, halved

sea salt

Preheat the oven to 200°C/180°C fan/Gas mark 6.

Cover the almonds with boiling water and leave for 5 minutes. One by one pinch the almonds, squeezing them out of their skins. Place the almonds on a baking tray and bake for 2 minutes in the oven. Remove and leave to cool.

Place the almonds in a food processor with the sourdough, garlic and 2 level teaspoons of sea salt, and blitz until very fine. When it is almost a paste, drizzle in the olive oil very slowly until the mixture is thick and smooth. Then slowly pour in the water and the sherry vinegar. Taste and adjust the seasoning if necessary, with a little more vinegar, salt or olive oil. Refrigerate for at least 2 hours, until thoroughly chilled. Taste again prior to serving, as the flavours will change slightly as they get to know each other in the fridge. The soup will also thicken as it cools, so you can add a few tablespoons of water if you want to thin it out a little. Ladle into chilled bowls and top with the grapes. Drizzle over a little more extra virgin olive oil and serve immediately.

smørrebrød

Smørrebrød is a staple open-faced sandwich on rye bread eaten across Denmark. It is most often piled high with things like smoked herring and rare beef as the main event – and all of them are delicious. Here though, I have included a list of ingredients that I most often use when making a quick lunch at home – they are not traditional toppings, but are just as enticing.

black multigrain seed bread (see page 52), or shop-bought rye bread

other ingredients to consider

butter

any pickled vegetables or gherkins, thinly sliced

kimchi and ferments

sea salt and pepper

instant pickled red onion

½ red onion, thinly sliced

1 tbsp red wine vinegar

my favourite combinations

- Rye, mayo (see aioli, page 134, omitting the garlic), lettuce, new potatoes, instant pickled red onion, chives

- Rye, mayo (see aioli, page 134, omitting the garlic), lettuce, soft-boiled egg, cherry tomatoes, capers

- Rye, labneh (page 216), smoked salmon, dill, sprouted grains/pulses (see page 169)

- Rye, mayo (see aioli, page 134, omitting the garlic), avocado, radish

to make instant pickled red onion

Place the sliced red onion in a bowl and combine with the red wine vinegar. Leave to pickle and colour for 20–30 minutes.

to cook new potatoes

Put the new potatoes in a saucepan of salted water and bring to the boil. Simmer for about 10 minutes, until just tender; a sharp knife should glide in without much resistance. Drain and leave to cool, then slice thickly and season well.

panzanella salad

serves 2

This is probably one of the most well-known recipes for using up stale bread – the vinegary tomato juices soak into the crusty loaf, bringing it back to life with a kick. Unsalted Tuscan bread would traditionally have been used, but sourdough is a really excellent option. Ripe, in-season tomatoes are essential here, and should be at room temperature. If you only have out-of-season, fridge-cold, anaemic-looking tomatoes don't bother with this salad, as the flavour will be lacking. Just wait until they are ripe, sweet and in season – it will be worth it.

While the consistency and flavour of the bread benefits from a brief period (10–20 minutes) sitting at room temperature once the salad has been made, don't be tempted to make it hours in advance, as it then moves into stodgy slop territory. Albeit rather nicely flavoured stodgy slop.

500g heritage tomatoes or baby plum tomatoes, or a combination

½ red onion, thinly sliced

1 garlic clove, crushed

100g roasted red pepper from a jar, torn into strips

1 tbsp capers, rinsed and drained

2½ tbsp red wine vinegar

2 tbsp extra virgin olive oil

2 thick slices of slightly stale spelt sourdough bread (see page 26, or shop bought)

small handful of flat-leaf parsley leaves

small bunch of basil leaves, roughly torn

sea salt and pepper

Cut the tomatoes into bite-size wedges or chunks, making sure to save all the juices. Put them in a bowl together with the onion, garlic, red pepper, capers, red wine vinegar, olive oil and a good pinch of salt and pepper.

Lightly toast the sourdough bread. (This is not traditional, but I like the addition of a slight crunch. Do try it untoasted as well, and decide how you like it.) Tear the bread into chunks, add to the salad with the parsley and most of the basil, and gently combine. Taste and adjust the seasoning with a little more vinegar, oil, salt or pepper if necessary.

Pile the salad on to a flat serving dish, scatter over the remaining basil leaves and leave to sit at room temperature for 10–20 minutes, so the bread has time to get acquainted with the other flavours, then serve.

sourdough French toast with avocado, tomato and labneh

Some people prefer to use brioche when it comes to French toast, but I like sourdough for its structure and flavour, and it doesn't become cloyingly sweet. I have gone for a savoury version here, but you can of course make it sweet – just leave out the salt and pepper and add a teaspoon of vanilla extract and half a teaspoon of ground cinnamon instead, then serve it up with any fruit you like and a good drizzle of maple syrup.

2 eggs

100ml thick coconut milk or cream

extra virgin coconut oil or butter, for frying

100g cherry tomatoes, halved

2 thick slices of spelt sourdough bread (see page 26, or shop bought)

labneh (see page 216, or Greek or coconut yoghurt), to serve

1 avocado, stoned and sliced

dried chilli flakes, to serve (optional)

extra virgin olive oil, to serve

sea salt and pepper

Beat together the eggs, coconut milk or cream, and a good pinch of salt and pepper.

Put 2 teaspoons of coconut oil or butter in a non-stick pan and set over a high heat. Add the tomatoes, season with a little salt and pepper and fry for 2 minutes until blistered. Place the tomatoes in a bowl, turn the heat down to medium and add another 1–2 teaspoons of oil or butter. Don't worry about cleaning out the pan, as the tomatoes will be going on top of the bread anyway.

Place the 2 slices of sourdough into the egg mixture, turning them over a few times so the bread absorbs the liquid. Put the soaked bread into the hot pan and fry for 2 minutes on each side, until golden.

Serve the bread with the labneh, tomatoes, avocado and dried chilli on top, if you like, and a little drizzle of olive oil.

pappa al pomodoro soup

serves 4

Don't let the simplicity of this humble tomato, bread and olive oil soup fool you; it has an incredible depth of flavour, and with the right ingredients it can be show-stopping. I make it in the summer when tomatoes are in season and bursting with sun-drenched sweetness; about 1kg is needed for four people, but if you prefer, you can halve this amount and top it up with one tin of tomatoes. Good-quality extra virgin olive oil is also necessary – ordinarily you would never cook with it, so it's important to go 'low and slow', as this preserves the beautifully fresh and vibrant flavour of the oil. Traditionally, the bread used would be quite stale, but I find sourdough is robust enough to be used fresh as well.

1kg ripe, sweet tomatoes – I find baby plum tomatoes work best

1 tbsp red wine or balsamic vinegar

extra virgin olive oil

1 onion, finely chopped

4 garlic cloves, crushed

60g spelt sourdough bread (see page 26, or shop bought)

small handful of basil, chopped, to serve

sea salt and pepper

Preheat the oven to 200°C/180°C fan/Gas mark 6.

Put the tomatoes in a baking tray, toss with the vinegar and 1 tablespoon of the oil, and season well with salt and pepper. Roast for 20 minutes, until the skins burst open and begin to caramelise.

Meanwhile, heat 4 tablespoons of the oil in a large saucepan over a low–medium heat. This may seem like a lot of oil, but it is important for the flavour of this soup. Add the onion and garlic and sweat them down until they are translucent, roughly the same time it takes for the tomatoes to roast. Make sure to keep the heat quite low otherwise the flavour of the extra virgin olive oil will be altered.

Blitz half of the roasted tomatoes and juices in a food processor or with a stick blender, until smooth. Add this and the whole tomatoes and all the oil and juices from the pan to the onions. Tear the bread into the pan and add most of the basil. Season with 1 teaspoon of salt and a grind of pepper, and simmer gently for 20 minutes. The soup should be very thick, but if it is too thick stir in a few tablespoons of water. Taste and adjust the seasoning if necessary.

Serve up in bowls with a good drizzle of extra virgin olive oil and the remaining basil scattered over the top.

ancient grains

We have the most incredible variety of grains available to us, yet more than half of the world's food energy comes from three 'mega crops' – rice, wheat and corn – which are bred for high-yield and industrial farming methods. This chapter showcases all the delicious dishes that can be made with alternative grains like farro, freekeh, amaranth, millet and teff, all of which are a good source of fibre, healthy fats, protein, vitamins and minerals. They are also all available in big supermarkets, or certainly in health-food shops and online. Alternatively, grains such as rye and barley can be used if you are having any difficulty tracking down the other grains.

a note on grains

While you may not be familiar with some of these grains, they are no more difficult to cook with, and certainly no less delicious than the mainstays such as rice or oats, so I would encourage you to get to know them. They also have a long shelf life so you don't have to use them all up in one go. Below are some of my favourites, I use them in salads, soups and stews, porridge and granola and when ground down into a flour they are wonderful in baking. For more information on grains and how our modern world is reliant on three main mega crops (wheat, rice and corn), refer to the IDRC (International Development Research Centre – https://www.idrc.ca).

grains – containing wheat/gluten

- Barley – originated in South East Asia and is most commonly sold as pearl barley, which has the outer husk and bran layers removed. See pearl barley with smashed cucumber, pomegranate and walnuts, page 182.

- Couscous – is a North African staple consisting of tiny balls of steamed semolina. It is incredibly quick to use. See couscous with broad beans and pecans, page 175.

- Bulgur wheat – is parboiled, then dried and cracked. It has an irregular shape and when cooked it has a delicious nutty flavour. It is perfect in place of couscous.

- Spelt – is a relative of wheat (see page 10). It originated in Iran and parts of southern Europe. It can be used whole, but takes a very long time to cook. So something like farro is preferable when used whole. However, when ground down to a flour, it has become extremely popular as an alternative to plain flour, because of its ease of use and reduced quantity of gluten.

- Farro – is the Italian name for Emmer wheat, a hard wheat grain that originated in Egypt. It is most commonly used in Italian cooking, and is loved for its chewy texture when cooked in soups, stews and as a grain in salads. See balsamic baked aubergines, mushrooms and farro, page 132.

- Kamut – is a trademark name given to a type of Khorasan grain. It is a brown grain, similar in appearance to brown basmati rice, with a nutty flavour and chewy texture when cooked. See roasted carrots with kamut, thyme, hazelnuts and garlic yoghurt, page 138.

- Freekeh – is an ancient Middle Eastern grain. It is actually wheat that has been harvested early, while still small and green in colour. The grain is roasted, then dried and rubbed, resulting in a slightly smoky, nutty flavour. See baked sweet potato and beetroot with roasted freekeh and salmoriglio, page 136.

- Rye – is a grain similar to wheat and barley and is widely used whole and ground down into a flour. See rye with cauliflower, peaches and tahini, page 176 and the rye and maple sourdough, page 36.

grains – without wheat/gluten

- Millet – is a small round grain native to Africa and Asia, with a slightly chewy consistency. See strawberry, millet, pistachios and goat's cheese, page 170.

- Oats – are naturally gluten free, but are often grown near to wheat, so if you are coeliac make sure to buy oats that are specifically labelled gluten free. See porridge sourdough, page 34 or oat and cherry pie, page 94.

- Amaranth – is not strictly speaking a grain but a tiny white seed discovered thousands of years ago by the Aztecs. See the quick red lentil and amaranth dhal, page 184.

- Buckwheat – originated in Asia and is a fruit seed related to rhubarb, with a unique triangular shape. It has a nutty flavour and is available roasted or unroasted. See the gluten-free chocolate, buckwheat and cardamom cake, page 78.

- Teff – is a miniscule African grain that comes in a variety of colours from white to red and dark brown. As a grain it is most often used to make a creamy porridge or as flour it is used to make the fermented flatbread injera, page 42.

soaking and sprouting

It is easy to forget that all grains are essentially dormant seeds, and we can bring them to life by soaking them, which triggers the germination process. This leads to the grains sprouting little tails, which would eventually grow into a plant given the right conditions – but is useful in the kitchen, too, as it neutralises the phytic acid present in their outer husks, which can interfere with the absorption of minerals like calcium, iron, zinc and magnesium. It also means the grains and pulses can now be eaten in their raw state, allowing for more minerals to be absorbed.

What I find really fascinating, though, is that soaking and sprouting has been a traditional method of preparing grains and pulses for generations – it was only overlooked fairly recently in pursuit of speed and efficiency. However, in countries like Korea, this simple method is still employed to this day – and I should say Korea is probably the most organised, fast-paced and efficient country I have ever worked in – so there are no excuses! Yes, it does take a little forethought, as you have to soak the grains the night before you use them, but very quickly it becomes an easy bedtime habit. Just throw a handful or two into a bowl, cover with water, and then you have a whole night and day to dream up all the delicious dishes to make with them.

soaking

Simply soaking grains for 12–24 hours will help to neutralise the phytic acid present in them. You can then cook them as you would usually, with the added bonus of them taking a shorter period of time to cook.

100g whole grains or pulses

Place the grains in a sieve and wash thoroughly under running water. Drain, transfer to a bowl and cover with a few inches of water. Cover the bowl and leave overnight.

sprouting

Sprouting just takes the soaking process a step further, so the grains can be eaten in their raw state, in salads, blended into smoothies or just as a snack.

You will need:
500ml jar
Muslin or a new J-cloth
Elastic band

Drain the grains that have been soaked overnight, rinse thoroughly, drain again, transfer to a glass jar, cover with muslin and secure with an elastic band. Invert the jar and place in a bowl resting against the side, so that excess water can drain out through the muslin and air can circulate into the jar. Leave at room temperature but out of direct sunlight.

Every morning and every evening, pour water into the jar to rinse the grains, then drain off the water completely and invert in a bowl as before. The grains will begin to sprout within 2–5 days, and will be ready to go once the tails have grown to 1–2cm in length. At this point, rinse and drain the grains thoroughly and refrigerate for up to 5–7 days. You will know they are past their best if they begin to go slimy.

strawberry, millet, pistachios and goat's cheese

serves 4

Millet is a very small, slightly chewy, nutty-flavoured seed that can be used in place of quinoa or couscous in most dishes. During the Middle Ages it was more popular than wheat – nowadays, however, it is most often seen in Asian and African cooking. It is also becoming increasingly popular among those who are seeking an alternative to grains containing gluten. Take note, it is sticky once cooked, so if you prefer a drier grain, use something like quinoa.

200g millet, quinoa or couscous – cooked according to packet instructions

350ml water

1½ tbsp balsamic vinegar

1 garlic clove, crushed

1 tsp maple syrup

zest of ½ unwaxed lemon

1 tbsp extra virgin olive oil

½ red onion, thinly sliced

80g pistachio nuts, shelled

150g strawberries, hulled and quartered

100g goat's cheese (optional)

70g rocket, lamb's lettuce or spinach, or a combination of the three

sea salt and pepper

Put the millet in a large, dry non-stick saucepan and set over a medium–high heat. Cook for 5 minutes, stirring frequently, until aromatic. The grains burn easily, so watch carefully. Add the water and ½ teaspoon salt, bring to the boil, then reduce the heat to medium–low, place the lid on top and simmer for about 10 minutes, or until all the water has been absorbed. Remove from the heat and leave to cool for another 10–15 minutes.

In a bowl, whisk together the vinegar, garlic, maple syrup, lemon zest and extra virgin olive oil. When the millet has cooled, pour over the dressing and gently combine, taking care not to mash up the millet, as it will lose its texture. Taste and adjust the seasoning if necessary.

Add the red onion, pistachios, strawberries and most of the goat's cheese, if using, and gently mix together. To serve, layer the salad leaves and millet on top of one another and finish with the remaining goat's cheese. The millet will be sticky, so you can use two spoons to make serving easier.

wild rice, apple, tomato and teff salad

serves 4

Wild rice retains an earthy bite after cooking, which is delicious here with the juicy apple and tomato. The teff is an optional extra for this salad, so don't be put off if you don't have it to hand – it is still delicious without it.

300g wild rice

20g mint leaves, plus extra to serve

50g rocket

2 garlic cloves

50g roasted pistachios or almonds

2 tbsp finely grated Parmesan or nutritional yeast

1 tbsp lemon juice

100ml extra virgin olive oil

50g teff (optional)

60ml water

2 small apples

300g mixture of cherry and heritage tomatoes, cut into bite-size chunks

handful of sprouted grains or pulses (see page 169, optional)

sea salt

Cook the wild rice according to the packet instructions.

While the rice is cooking, make the dressing. Put the mint, rocket, garlic, pistachios or almonds into a food processor and blitz until you have a paste. Add the Parmesan or nutritional yeast, lemon juice, 1 tablespoon of water, ¼ teaspoon of salt and the olive oil, and blitz until smooth and well combined. As soon as the rice is cooked, drain well and, while still hot, pour over the dressing and combine. Taste and adjust the seasoning if necessary.

If you are using the teff, put it in a dry saucepan and set it over a medium heat. Cook for 2–3 minutes, stirring frequently, until aromatic and you can hear the grains popping. Cover with 60ml of water and a pinch of salt. Turn the heat down to the lowest setting and cook gently for 6–8 minutes, until all the water has been absorbed. Remove from the heat, cover and leave to steam for about 10 minutes.

Core the apples and slice into thin wedges. Add most of the tomatoes and apples to the rice and combine. Serve on a platter with the remaining apple, tomato and mint on top. If using, scatter over the teff and sprouted grains. This is lovely at room temperature, and keeps well for a day or so.

couscous with broad beans and pecans

serves 4

This is a really quick and simple recipe, but the preserved lemon and pecans pack in great flavour, making this one of my favourite salads. You can use quinoa here instead of the couscous, and if you want to beef it up even further you can serve it with grilled fish or meaty vegetables. It's summer on a plate really. A little bit of the garlic yoghurt (page 228) or miso tahini (page 219) drizzled over the top is also delicious!

320g couscous

400ml boiling water

¼ preserved lemon (see page 210 or shop bought), flesh removed and finely chopped

5 tbsp extra virgin olive oil, plus extra to drizzle

350g fresh podded broad beans, or frozen

30g mint, roughly chopped

20g parsley, roughly chopped

150g cherry tomatoes, halved

100g pecans, roasted

6 cloves garlic confit, see page 220 (optional)

2 tbsp pomegranate molasses

Sea salt and pepper

Put the couscous into a large, wide bowl. Stir ½ teaspoon of sea salt into the boiling water and pour over the couscous. Leave the couscous to soak up the liquid for 5–10 minutes, then fluff with a fork and stir in the preserved lemon and 4 tablespoons of the extra virgin olive oil.

Bring a pot of water to the boil and add 2 teaspoons salt. Add the broad beans and cook for 3–4 minutes, until just tender. Drain and refresh under cold water. You can leave the broad beans as they are, or remove their outer skins to reveal their vibrant green inner shell. It's not the most scintillating kitchen exercise, but it's worth it for the colour.

In a large bowl, gently but thoroughly mix together the couscous, broad beans, most of the chopped herbs, the tomatoes and most of the pecans and the garlic confit, if using. Add the molasses and the remaining tablespoon of the extra virgin olive oil. Taste and adjust the seasoning if necessary with a little more salt and pepper.

Serve on a large dish with the remaining herbs and pecans sprinkled on top.

rye with cauliflower, peaches and tahini

**serves 2, or
4 as a side**

The gentle sweetness of the peaches with the earthy rye and cauliflower works so well – and the tahini sauce makes the combination almost addictive! This keeps well for a few days if you add the peaches in at the last moment to ensure they stay fresh.

250g rye grain, soaked overnight in plenty of water, or 450g ready-to-eat rye, spelt or barley

150ml tahini verde (see page 218)

2 tsp soy sauce

350g cauliflower florets

3 tbsp rapeseed or olive oil

sea salt and pepper

2 peaches or nectarines, stoned and cut into wedges

50g toasted flaked almonds, to serve

2 tbsp mint and parsley leaves, to serve

Preheat the oven to 200°C/180°C fan/Gas mark 6.

If you have soaked raw rye grain, drain it in a sieve, then transfer it to a large saucepan. Cover with plenty of water and bring to the boil. Reduce the heat and simmer for 45–55 minutes. The grains should be cooked through, but still a little chewy. Drain and transfer to a bowl. While still hot add the tahini verde and soy sauce, and combine. Set aside. If you are using ready-to-eat rye, spelt or barley, heat it up according to the packet instructions, then combine with the tahini verde and soy sauce as above.

While the rye is cooking, toss the cauliflower with the oil in a baking tray and season generously with salt and pepper. Roast for 15 minutes, until it is golden and a sharp knife glides into the thickest part of the floret.

To serve, combine the rye with the cauliflower and peaches or nectarines and scatter over the flaked almonds and herbs.

camargue red rice with squash and cavolo nero

serves 4

The earthy, nutty and chewy consistency of Camargue rice from southern France is incredibly satisfying, and works very well in salads, absorbing all the flavours of whatever dressing you choose. A short-grain brown rice would also work very well here.

400g onion or butternut squash, halved, deseeded and cut into 1cm-thick slices – no need to peel

1 red onion, cut into wedges

4 garlic cloves, peeled

6 tbsp extra virgin olive oil

1¼ tsp sweet smoked paprika

250g Camargue red rice

150g cavolo nero, stalks removed and leaves roughly chopped

1½ tbsp pomegranate molasses

2 tsp balsamic vinegar

sea salt and pepper

Preheat the oven to 200°C/180°C fan/Gas mark 6, and put a large saucepan of salted water on to boil.

Toss the squash, onion and garlic with 2 tablespoons of the olive oil and 1 teaspoon of the paprika and season generously. Roast for 20–25 minutes, until just tender and golden.

By the time you are putting the vegetables into the oven, the water should be boiling. Add in the rice and simmer for about 20 minutes, until cooked. It should still be a bit chewy. Strain off the water and leave the rice to dry out in the warm pot.

While the vegetables and rice are cooking, put 1 tablespoon of olive oil into a large frying pan and set over a high heat. When hot, add the cavolo nero and fry for 5–6 minutes, turning frequently, until the leaves are crispy and slightly charred. Remove and set aside.

When the vegetables are cooked, put the roasted garlic in a bowl and mash with a fork. Add in the remaining ¼ teaspoon of smoked paprika, the pomegranate molasses, balsamic vinegar and remaining 3 tablespoons of olive oil. Whisk to combine, then pour over the rice and stir through. Taste and adjust the seasoning if necessary.

On a large serving dish, layer the rice with the squash, onions and kale. Serve immediately.

Buddha bowl with squash, ginger, cucumber, avocado and seaweed

serves 4

I stayed in a Buddhist monastery in Korea, where the rituals around the preparation and eating of food were fascinating. To begin with you were presented with a set of bowls and eating utensils wrapped in linen, which had to be unwrapped and laid out in a very specific order. Food was then offered to you, but you had to make sure you only served yourself an amount that you could finish, as it was forbidden to leave even a grain of rice behind. When you finished your meal, you would rinse your bowls and utensils with a little water, and then drink this rinsing water, so that you left no trace of your meal at all. The idea behind this is to encourage a greater awareness of what our bodies truly need, to limit excess and to be fully present as we eat each mouthful of food. While our busy modern lives may not allow for such a ritualistic and ordered approach to eating, the idea of mindfulness and taking a brief moment before and after our meals to fully appreciate and be thankful for all that we have is certainly something we can strive for. Strictly speaking, the spring onions and ginger that I have used here are breaking the rules, as it is believed they will incite the libido . . . but as I am not a Buddhist monk I am willing to take that risk!

300g short-grain brown rice

toppings

500g onion or butternut squash, peeled, deseeded and cut into bite-sized chunks

2 ripe avocados, halved, stoned, skin removed and sliced

Cook the rice according to the packet instructions. Put the squash chunks in a sieve positioned inside a saucepan filled with a little water, making sure that the water does not touch the bottom of the sieve (or a steamer if you have one). Place a lid over the squash and set the pan over a high heat. Steam the squash for 15 minutes, until a knife glides in easily. Alternatively, you can roast the squash.

100g cucumber or cucumber ferment (see page 250), thinly sliced

4 spring onions, thinly sliced

25g pickled ginger or carrot, apple and ginger pickle (see page 242), thinly sliced

4 tbsp sprouted grains or pulses, (see page 169, optional)

1 tbsp roasted sesame seeds

2 sheets of roasted crispy seaweed, thinly sliced with scissors

dressing (the kimchi salsa verde on page 212 is also delicious with this)

1 tsp wasabi paste

2 tbsp tamari or soy sauce

1 tbsp mirin

1 tsp Korean doenjang or Japanese miso paste

juice of ½ lime

1 tsp honey

For the dressing, mix all the ingredients together in a bowl until combined.

Divide the cooked rice between 4 bowls and arrange the toppings over the rice. Spoon the dressing over the top, and serve immediately.

pearl barley with smashed cucumber, pomegranate and walnuts

serves 4

This is a delicious and hearty salad all on its own, but it also works well as a side dish alongside pretty much any meat or fish. I adore roasting cucumber – it gives it a completely different flavour – and if you happen to have the weather for a BBQ, then by all means fling the cucumber on the grill to blister and char to perfection.

300g pearl barley

1 large cucumber

1 tbsp olive oil

small bunch each of mint and parsley, finely chopped

seeds of 1 pomegranate

60g walnuts, roughly broken

sea salt and pepper

mint yoghurt, to serve (see page 228)

dressing

2 tsp cumin seeds

3 tbsp extra virgin olive oil

1 tbsp pomegranate molasses

1½ tbsp balsamic vinegar

zest of 1 unwaxed lemon

Preheat the oven to 220°C/200°C fan/Gas mark 7.

Bring a large saucepan of salted water to the boil, add the barley and simmer briskly for 25–30 minutes, until the barley is cooked through but still al dente.

Meanwhile, gently bash the cucumber with a rolling pin or tin of beans, until it cracks open and breaks into rough shapes. Transfer the cucumber to a baking tray and toss it with the olive oil, then season with salt and pepper. Roast for 15 minutes until slightly charred.

For the dressing, fry the cumin seeds in a dry frying pan over a medium–high heat for 2–3 minutes, until they are a shade darker and aromatic. Take care not to burn them. Place them in a bowl and combine with the rest of the ingredients.

When the barley is cooked, drain well, transfer to a bowl and combine with the dressing and most of the mint, parsley, pomegranate seeds and walnuts.

Layer the barley and cucumber on a serving platter, and scatter over the remaining herbs, pomegranate and nuts. Serve with the mint yoghurt.

quick red lentil and amaranth dhal with courgette and tomato

serves 4

I turn to this dish on those achingly cold winter days when I want to eat something deeply warming and comforting like a slow-cooked stew, but have neither the time nor the inclination to cook one. This dhal comes together in under half an hour, but lacks none of the cosy goodness of its 'low and slow' brethren. Amaranth is a tiny seed, but don't be put off by its diminutive size, as it packs a nutritional punch – with more protein than oats, it is also a good source of Omega-3 fats, iron, calcium, vitamin B, magnesium and zinc. If you don't have them to hand, just replace with more lentils.

220g split red lentils

40g amaranth, or more lentils

5 cloves garlic, crushed

2 tbsp tamari or soy sauce

1 tsp ground coriander

1 tsp ground cumin

775ml of water

50ml yoghurt (dairy, soy or coconut), plus extra to serve

2 tbsp olive oil, plus extra to drizzle (optional)

1 courgette, halved lengthways and sliced

200g baby plum tomatoes, halved

small handful of coriander, chopped, to serve

sea salt and pepper

Wash the lentils and amaranth thoroughly under running water. Transfer them to a large saucepan together with the garlic, tamari or soy sauce, and ground coriander and cumin, and cover with the water. Bring to the boil, reduce the heat and simmer for 15 minutes, stirring frequently to stop the lentils sticking to the base of the pan. Add the yoghurt and simmer for another 5 minutes until you have a creamy dhal.

While the lentils and amaranth are cooking, put the oil in a pan and place over a high heat. Add the courgette and tomatoes, season with salt and pepper and fry for 3–4 minutes, until slightly golden and charred. Turn off the heat and leave to one side.

When the dhal has finished cooking, divide it between 4 bowls, top with the courgette, tomato, coriander and a dollop of yoghurt. Drizzle over a little olive oil if you like, and serve immediately.

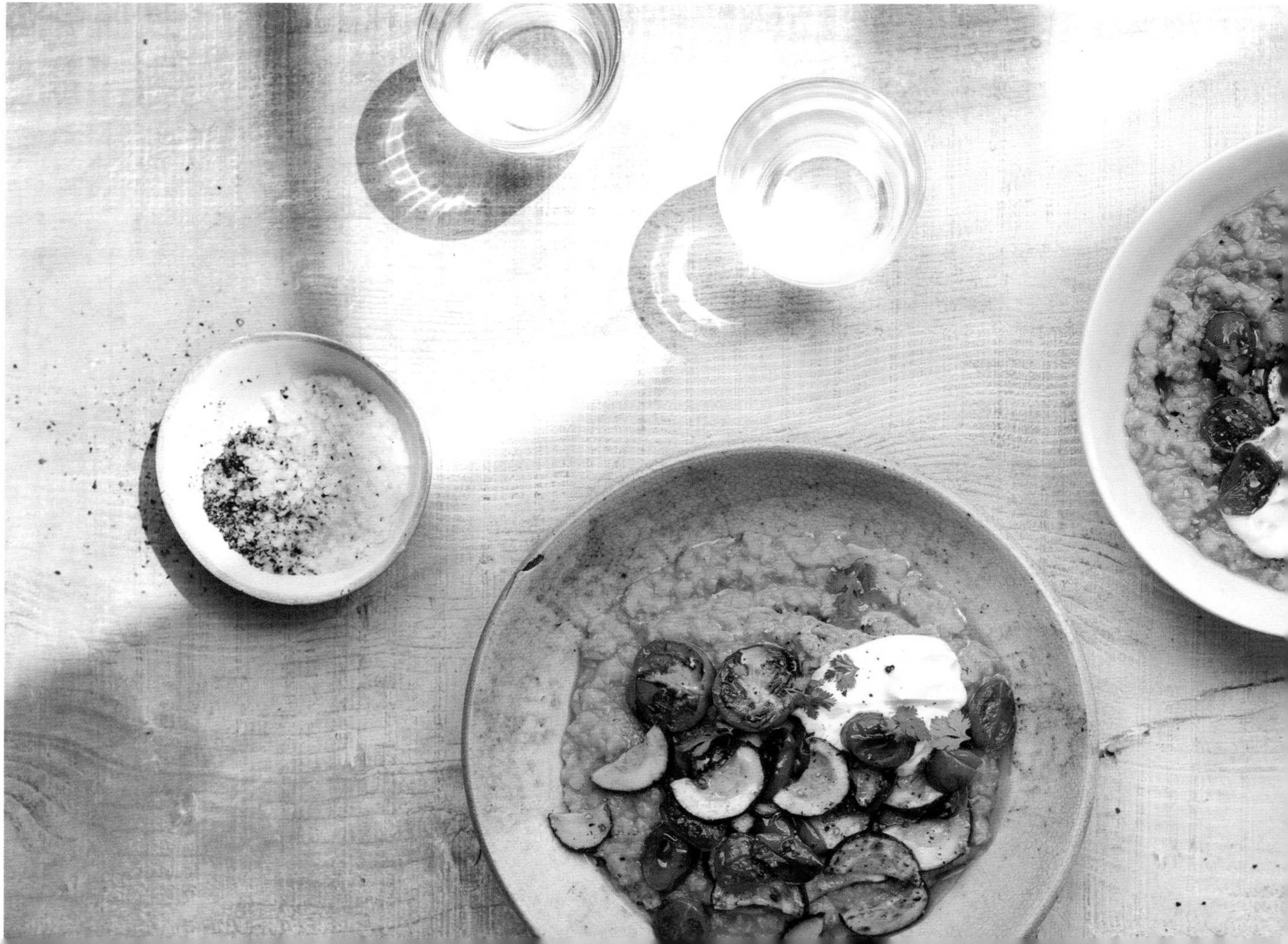

puy lentil and freekeh
soup with chorizo

serves 6

Nourishing and filling with all the vegetables, lentils and freekeh, this soup will easily power you through from lunch to dinner. If you want to make it vegetarian, use vegetable stock and substitute smoked tofu for the chorizo. A poached egg on top is not a bad idea either.

3 tbsp olive oil

1 onion, finely chopped

3 celery sticks, chopped

1 red pepper, deseeded and roughly chopped

4 garlic cloves, crushed

250g baby plum tomatoes, halved

½ tsp sweet smoked paprika

2 sprigs of rosemary, leaves removed and finely chopped

150g puy lentils

150g freekeh

2 litres fresh chicken or vegetable stock

150g spinach

100g chorizo, thinly sliced

small handful of flat-leaf parsley, chopped to serve

6 poached eggs, to serve (optional)

sea salt and pepper

Put the olive oil in a large saucepan and set it over a medium heat. When hot, add the onion, celery and red pepper. Sweat for 10 minutes, until the onion is translucent. Add the garlic, tomatoes, paprika and rosemary and cook for another 5 minutes. Add the lentils, freekeh and stock, bring to the boil, reduce the heat and simmer for 25–30 minutes, until the lentils and freekeh are cooked through but still retain a little bite. Season to taste with salt and pepper. Bear in mind that if you used instant stock you may not need any salt at all. If you used fresh unsalted stock you may need up to a teaspoon of salt. Stir in the spinach and cook for 1–2 minutes, until wilted down.

Meanwhile, fry the chorizo in a dry frying pan over a medium heat until crispy. Set aside, together with any rendered oil.

Serve in bowls, with the chorizo and parsley scattered over and the poached egg positioned in the centre, if you like.

mushroom and farro soup

serves 6–8

I spend a month or so working in Korea each year, and when I come home I really crave all their delicious soups and stews, in particular one called doenjang jjigae. Doenjang is a Korean fermented miso paste, similar to Japanese miso but with much more depth of flavour. It can transform otherwise dull soups and stews in seconds, so I use it a lot when I don't have any stock to hand. This is a hearty soup, perfect for a filling and healthy lunch.

20g dried porcini mushrooms

1 x 10cm piece dried kombu seaweed, optional

2 litres of water

3 tbsp olive oil

4 carrots, peeled and chopped into 1cm dice

2 onions, chopped

2 celery sticks, chopped into 1cm dice

300g mixed fresh mushrooms (Portobello, shiitake, etc.), thickly sliced

4 garlic cloves, crushed

2 tbsp Korean doenjang soya bean paste, or miso paste

100g farro

4 sprigs of thyme

2 tsp tamari or soy sauce, to taste

sea salt and pepper

small handful of flat-leaf parsley, roughly chopped, to serve

Put the porcini and kombu into a large saucepan and cover them with the water. Slowly bring to the boil, then reduce the temperature and simmer gently for 20 minutes. Remove any scum that comes to the surface.

Meanwhile, put the oil in another large saucepan and set over a medium heat. When hot, add the carrots, onions, celery and fresh mushrooms and sweat gently for 10 minutes, until the onions are translucent. Add the garlic and doenjang or miso, and cook for another 2 minutes.

Remove the kombu from the mushroom stock. Transfer the porcini and all the cooking liquid into the pan of cooked vegetables together with the farro and thyme. Bring to the boil, then reduce the heat and simmer for 20–30 minutes, until the farro is tender but still chewy. Taste and, if necessary, season with a little tamari or soy sauce.

Serve in bowls with the parsley sprinkled over.

black rice and coconut milk porridge

serves 2

I eat Irish oats almost every morning of the year in one form or another. There is something about that hour of the day that requires the minimum of decision-making and fuss. While oats are of course delicious and sustaining, I do sometimes feel I should be more adventurous with my morning meal and try out something different every now and again. When I do, this black rice porridge is a favourite. I soak the rice the night before, as it reduces the cooking time and improves the consistency.

100g black rice, soaked in plenty of cold water overnight

250ml coconut milk, plus more to drizzle

Pinch sea salt

1 tsp vanilla extract or paste

100ml of water

Fruit of your choice for topping – berries, mango, banana, etc.

Roasted nuts of your choice – almonds, cashews, pecans, etc.

Maple syrup (optional)

Drain and rince the rice and transfer it to a large saucepan together with the coconut milk, salt, vanilla and water. Bring to the boil, then reduce the temperature and simmer gently for 35–40 minutes, stirring every now and again until the rice is cooked through, chewy and slightly creamy.

Divide the rice between 2 bowls and top with your chosen fruit and nuts. Drizzle over the extra coconut milk and maple syrup if you like some extra sweetness, although I find the fruit is usually enough.

beghrir pancakes with nectarines and honey

makes about
12 pancakes

I first encountered these ancient Berber semolina pancakes in Fez, Morocco, where they are eaten for breakfast or as a light snack with warm honey, yoghurt and fresh or dried fruit. Beghrir, or 'thousand hole', pancakes are cooked only on one side so they have a very distinctive appearance, almost like a loofah sponge, ideal for soaking up whatever toppings you have to hand. These pancakes require proving time, so make the batter the night before and it'll be ready to go in the morning.

300ml lukewarm water

1 tsp maple syrup

10g fresh yeast or
4g instant yeast

130g fine semolina flour

130g white spelt flour

½ tsp sea salt

1 egg

1 tsp baking powder

70ml milk (dairy, rice
or almond), gently
warmed in a saucepan
until lukewarm

½ tsp rapeseed or
sunflower oil, to fry

2 tbsp extra virgin
coconut oil or butter

4 tbsp honey

2 nectarines, stoned
and sliced into wedges
(or other stone fruit of
your choice)

Yoghurt (Greek, soy
or coconut), to serve

1 tbsp pistachio nuts,
to scatter

Put the warm water, maple syrup and yeast in a blender and leave it to sit in a warm place (without turning it on) for 10–15 minutes, until the yeast dissolves and becomes frothy.

Add both flours, the salt, egg, baking powder and lukewarm milk to the blender and blend for about 1 minute, until the mixture is smooth. Pour the mixture into a bowl, cover with a tea towel and leave in a warm place to prove for about 1½–2 hours, until the mixture has increased in size and is very bubbly. You can make the pancakes at this point, or cover the mixture and refrigerate overnight.

When you're ready to cook, heat a non-stick frying pan with the rapeseed or sunflower oil over a medium–high heat. Stir the mixture, and when the pan is hot pour a small ladleful of batter on to the centre of the pan, until it is about 10–12cm in diameter. Reduce the heat to the lowest setting and cook gently (without flipping) until the top is bubbly and completely dry and the base is golden. Place the pancake on a plate and keep covered with a tea towel in a low oven (50°C or the lowest temperature setting available) to keep warm while you cook the remaining pancakes.

When you are ready to serve, mix the coconut oil and honey in a small saucepan over a medium heat, until combined. (In Morocco they would traditionally use butter, but I love the flavour combination of the honey and coconut oil. Of course, you can use butter if you prefer.)

Serve with the nectarine wedges, honey mixture, a dollop of yoghurt and the pistachios.

overnight sweet potato oats

serves 2

This was a happy accident – leftover whole roast sweet potato from dinner, and oats that I had soaking overnight. Combine them together and you have a delicious and nourishing start to your day.

2 sweet potatoes, about 450g

130g rolled oats

260ml almond or rice milk, plus extra to serve

1 tsp vanilla extract

½ tsp ground cinnamon (optional)

pinch of sea salt

4 tbsp yoghurt (Greek, coconut or soy)

2 tbsp roasted almonds, cut into slivers

2 tsp maple syrup (optional)

Preheat the oven to 200°C/180°C fan/Gas mark 6.

Wrap the sweet potatoes in foil and bake for 40 minutes, until the flesh is completely soft. Remove from the oven and leave to cool.

Meanwhile, in a large bowl, combine the oats, milk, vanilla, cinnamon and salt. Once the potatoes are cool enough to handle, cut them in half, scoop out the flesh and mash it to a pulp with a fork. Add this to the oat mixture and stir to combine. Cover and refrigerate overnight.

The following morning, stir the oats. The mixture will be quite thick; if you prefer it a little thinner, add in a tablespoon or 2 of almond milk, and combine. Divide the oats between 2 bowls and top with the yoghurt, almonds and a little drizzle of maple syrup if you like.

rye, barley and oat
bircher muesli

serves 6

If you are making bread at home you are likely to have a lot of rye, spelt and barley flakes in your cupboards. The good news is, they can be used in the same way as oats to make a delicious bircher muesli. Of course if you don't have them, just replace them with the same quantity of oats.

50g rye flakes

50g barley flakes

200g jumbo oats

2 apples, cored and grated

300ml almond or rice milk

200ml fresh apple or orange juice

50g raisins or dried apricots, chopped

50g dried cranberries

1 tbsp maple syrup, plus extra to drizzle

150g mixed seeds – pumpkin, sunflower, linseed, etc.

1½ tsp ground cinnamon

400g yoghurt (Greek, coconut or soy)

any other fruit, nuts and seeds, to serve

In a large bowl mix together all the ingredients apart from the yoghurt. Cover and leave to soak overnight in the fridge.

In the morning, stir in the yoghurt and serve in bowls with any fruit, nuts and seeds you like. Drizzle over a little more maple syrup or a sprinkle of cinnamon if you wish. Alternatively, you can serve the oats in large glass jam jars with layers of yoghurt and fruit for breakfast on the go.

baked oats with mango, blueberries and banana

serves 4

I usually make this on the weekend, as it takes about 40 minutes to bake, which seems a bit ambitious on a weekday morning. The fruit here can easily be swapped for any others you prefer.

150g rolled oats

60g almonds, halved

1 tsp baking powder

1 tsp ground cinnamon

½ tsp fine sea salt

240ml almond milk

60ml maple syrup

1 egg

1½ tsp vanilla extract

1 mango, peeled, stoned and flesh cut into cubes

2 bananas, peeled and sliced

150g blueberries and strawberries, sliced

yoghurt (Greek, soy or coconut), to serve (optional)

18–20cm round or square casserole dish or cake tin

Preheat the oven to 190°C/170°C fan/Gas mark 5, and grease the dish or tin.

In a bowl, combine the oats, almonds, baking powder, cinnamon and salt. In another bowl combine the milk, maple syrup, egg, vanilla and chopped mango flesh. Add the the dry mix to the wet and thoroughly combine.

Place a layer of bananas, then a layer of berries on the base of the casserole dish or cake tin and cover with half the oat mixture, then the remaining fruit and oat mix. Bake for 35–40 minutes, until set and golden. Leave to cool for 10 minutes, then spoon out into bowls and serve immediately, with yoghurt if you like.

spelt and hemp seed granola

**makes about
10 portions**

If speed is your number-one priority when it comes
to breakfast, then cook up a batch of this granola
and you'll be ready to go all week long. It is leagues
better for you than any commercial breakfast cereal,
and tastes better too I bet. Granola is very flexible,
so if you only have oats that is fine, and pretty much
any nuts and seeds will do too. Just stick to the same
weights, and it will be perfect. Don't be tempted
to turn up the heat to speed up the cooking time,
though, as you will end up with acrid-tasting granola.

200g jumbo oats

200g spelt flakes, or
more jumbo oats

80g shelled hemp seeds

60g pecan nuts

60g pumpkin seeds

¼ tsp ground cinnamon

zest of 1 unwaxed lemon

zest of ½ an orange
(optional)

¼ tsp fine sea salt

120ml brown rice
syrup or maple syrup

120ml extra virgin
coconut oil, melted

150g dried apricots,
chopped

Preheat the oven to 160°C/140°C fan/Gas mark 3.

In a large mixing bowl combine the oats, spelt flakes,
hemp seeds, pecans, pumpkin seeds, cinnamon, lemon
zest, orange zest and salt.

Pour over the brown rice syrup and melted coconut
oil and combine thoroughly until everything is well
coated. Divide the mixture between 2 baking sheets
and bake for 30 minutes, stirring every 10 minutes
or so, until golden. Bear in mind that the granola
will not be crispy when hot, so don't be tempted to
keep baking it. Remove from the oven and combine
with the chopped dried apricots, and leave to cool
completely. Transfer to a glass jar or resealable
container, and keep for up to 2 weeks.

preserves, dressings and oils

Jams, compotes, chutneys, herb oils and spice pastes are just some of the glorious ways to lift a dish from dull to exciting – and this chapter shows you how. From rhubarb marmalade, citrus curd and preserved lemons to kimchi salsa verde, thyme and rosemary salmoriglio and flavoured oils, it would be very hard to find a dish that would not benefit from one of these lovely condiments.

rhubarb marmalade

makes 2 x 250g jars

My dad is old-school Irish, so scones get at least a centimetre-thick slathering of good salted butter (Irish butter, naturally), and on top of that, a dollop of thick-cut marmalade. He powers through the stuff at an alarming rate, so it is our go-to airport panic buy when we're en route back home to Ireland. Making marmalade at home is of course pretty straightforward, but this version jazzes things up slightly with rhubarb added to it, and honey used instead of cane sugar, which I prefer both for its floral notes and the fact that it is less refined. It does mean the marmalade will not set into a hard gel or last for years on end, like some sugar-laden jams, but that is no bad thing in my book. With this in mind I make it in smaller batches that last a month or two in the fridge, by which time you will have polished them off anyway, so there's no fear of any remaining jars going bad. If you use forced rhubarb the marmalade will take on a lovely pink hue – otherwise it will be more like it is here in the photo.

3 Seville oranges (about 550g preferably organic)

½ unwaxed lemon

50ml water

300ml honey

325g rhubarb stalks, chopped into 2cm chunks

2 x 250g glass jar with a lid, sterilised

Using a peeler, peel the zest off the oranges in long, thick strips, then cut the strips into thin slices. If they are very long, cut them into halves or quarters, so they are 2–3cm in length. Juice the oranges and the lemon into a large heavy-based pot, reserving the pips and any pith and skin. Wrap these in a piece of muslin and secure with string. Put this into the pot together with the slivers of orange zest. Add the water, bring to the boil then simmer gently for 60–90 minutes, or until the zest is soft. Remove the muslin bag and leave to cool in a bowl.

preserves, dressings and oils

Once cool, squeeze as much of the juice out of the muslin bag as possible and add this to the pot, together with the honey and rhubarb. Bring the mixture back to the boil, then reduce the temperature and simmer for 20–30 minutes, or until the mixture is thick and gelatinous.

Transfer to sterilised jars, seal and leave to cool completely. Store in the fridge for up to 2 months.

spiced raisin jam

makes 2 x
250g jars

This is basically Christmas pudding in a jar. It is rich
and fragrant – perfect on a scone or oatcake (see page
66), or on some toasted sourdough of course.

2 oranges

150g raisins

150g sultanas

200g coconut
palm sugar

100g honey

1 tbsp soy sauce

1 tbsp rice vinegar

1 tsp ground coriander

2 x 250g glass jar
with a lid, sterilised

Zest 1 of the oranges and keep the zest to one side.
Peel both oranges and chop the segments into chunks.
Discard the skin.

Place the orange pieces in a saucepan together with
the rest of the ingredients and bring to the boil,
stirring frequently. Reduce the heat to a gentle simmer
and continue to cook for 20–25 minutes, stirring now
and again, until the mixture has thickened a little.
Remove from the heat and stir through the zest.

Transfer to sterilised jam jars and seal while still hot.
Leave to cool completely, then store in the fridge for
up to 4 months.

strawberry, balsamic and thyme jam

**makes 1 x
250g jar**

This is a cinch to make, and the balsamic and thyme work really well with the strawberries, so don't be put off! This is not a traditional jam – really it is just stewed fruit, so it will last for about 2 weeks in the fridge – but between my wife and me it never lasts that long. Double or triple the recipe if you wish.

**500g strawberries,
hulled and halved**

125g coconut palm sugar

1 tbsp balsamic vinegar

1½ tsp thyme leaves

**1 x 250g glass jar with
a lid, sterilised**

Put all of the ingredients into a large, heavy-based saucepan and set over a medium–low heat. Simmer for 30–40 minutes, until the sugar is fully dissolved and the fruit has stewed down and become thick.

Pour into a sterilised jar, seal and leave to cool completely. Refrigerate for up to 2 weeks.

citrus curd of lemon and orange

makes 2 x
250g jars

The colour and glorious citrus flavour of this curd just screams of summer. This is a really simple recipe for a more healthful, but no less bright and delicious lemon and orange curd, made using honey instead of cane sugar, which lends the curd a floral note. I also give you the option of using coconut oil, which is a delicious alternative to butter if you are so inclined. This is lovely just as it is on some crunchy toasted bread, stirred into yoghurt, or added to icing for cakes and whatever else you fancy.

zest and juice of 2
unwaxed lemons

zest of 1 orange

200g set honey

80g extra virgin coconut
oil or unsalted butter

2 eggs, beaten

2 x 250g glass jar with
a lid, sterilised

Put all the ingredients, apart from the eggs, into a heatproof bowl set over a pan of gently simmering water, ensuring that the base of the bowl does not touch the water. Stir the mixture until the oil and honey melt down.

Mix in the eggs, whisking constantly until fully incorporated, making sure the heat is not too high or the eggs will scramble. Cook the mixture for 10–12 minutes, stirring frequently, until the curd is thick and creamy.

Remove from the heat and leave to cool completely, then transfer to the sterlisied jars, cover and keep refrigerated for up to 2 months.

chilli tomato jam

makes 3–4 x
250g jars

This is a great all-rounder – perfect with vegetables, meat or fish or as a savoury note on toast, or slathered on to a sandwich as you would chutney.

2 tsp cumin seeds

2 tsp mustard seeds

2 red onions,
finely chopped

800g ripe cherry/baby
plum tomatoes, halved

2 red chillies, deseeded
and finely chopped

15g fresh ginger, peeled
and finely grated

3 garlic cloves, crushed

150g coconut palm sugar

75ml red wine vinegar

1 tbsp fish sauce

3–4 x 250g glass jar
with a lid, sterilised

Put the cumin and mustard seeds in a dry frying pan over a medium heat. Cook for 3–4 minutes, until they are aromatic and the mustard seeds start popping. Take care not to let them burn. Remove the seeds and crush them to a powder using a pestle and mortar or coffee grinder.

Put the ground seeds in a large saucepan with the rest of the ingredients, apart from the fish sauce. Bring to the boil, then reduce the heat and simmer for 30–40 minutes, until very thick and viscous. Add in the fish sauce and cook for another few minutes. Transfer to sterilised jam jars and seal while still hot. Leave to cool completely then store in the fridge for up to 6–8 weeks.

preserved lemons

makes 1 x 1 litre jar, or 6 large preserved lemons

Yes, it takes almost a month before you can use them ... but in the time it takes you to decide whether or not you want to wait that long, you could have actually made them! So rather than thinking about it, just do it, pop them in the fridge and then in a month's time the pay-off begins. Think zingy salads, tagines, spiced yoghurts, flavoured oils – the list goes on. Once they have had their month or so of preservation, all you have to do is slice them in half and remove the flesh, then finely slice the skin and add it to whatever dish you are making. I have also preserved bergamots – the greeny-yellow citrus fruit – which have a beautifully floral note to them. So feel free to experiment.

10 organic unwaxed lemons

7 tbsp sea salt

2 sprigs of thyme (optional)

1 x 1-litre glass jar with a lid, sterilised

Wash and dry the lemons. One at a time, stand 6 of the lemons on 1 end and, with a sharp knife, cut the lemon lengthways into quarters, making sure you do not cut all the way through, leaving about 1.5cm of the base intact, to keep the quarters together. Set the remaining lemons aside.

Add 1 tablespoon of the salt to the base of the jar. Over a bowl, stuff each cut lemon with 1 tablespoon of salt, then transfer them to the jar together with any juice and salt that fell into the bowl. Pack them in as tightly as possible so that the lemon juice is released into the jar. Add the thyme, seal the jar and leave in a cool, dark place for 4 days.

After this time, squeeze as many of the remaining 4 lemons as needed to top up the jar with lemon juice. Seal the jar again and refrigerate for 3–4 weeks, upending the jar once a week to redistribute the salt.

To serve, rinse off any excess salt and cut away the flesh, then slice up the peel as required.

kimchi salsa verde

makes about 400g

Kimchi works in much the same way as capers and anchovies do in the traditional salsa verde, adding a delicious sharpness and depth of flavour that grounds all the other flavours and brings them together. I use this sauce on everything – salads, grains, lentils, fish, meat, slathered on toasted sourdough . . . anything!

30g flat-leaf parsley
leaves, finely chopped

15g basil leaves,
finely chopped

10g mint leaves,
finely chopped

1.5 tbsp capers, rinsed

4 tbsp kimchi (see page
246 or shop bought),
finely chopped

1 shallot, finely chopped

zest of 1 unwaxed lemon

1 tbsp Dijon mustard

240ml extra virgin
olive oil

2 tbsp red wine vinegar

sea salt and pepper

2 x 250g glass jar with
a lid, sterilised

In a large bowl, combine the chopped herbs, capers, kimchi, shallot, lemon zest and mustard. Drizzle in the oil, and combine. Season with salt and pepper to taste. Just before serving, add the red wine vinegar, taste and adjust the seasoning if necessary.

Transfer to your sterilised jars, which you can keep in the fridge for 1–2 months.

preserves, dressings and oils

harissa

This North African pepper and chilli sauce adds a perfumed kick to pretty much anything, be it roast vegetables, grilled fish or slathered on to a sandwich like the Turkish mackerel sourdough sandwich, page 150. It keeps well in an airtight container in the fridge for up to one month, so you can double the recipe if you are a fan.

2 tsp coriander seeds

2 tsp cumin seeds

2 tsp caraway seeds

4 tbsp extra virgin olive oil

1 red onion, finely chopped

2 red chillies, deseeded and finely chopped

3 garlic cloves, crushed

4 piquillo peppers or 1 roasted red pepper (shop bought in a jar)

3 tsp tomato purée

2 tbsp lemon juice

1 tsp sweet smoked paprika

sea salt and pepper

1 x 200g glass jar with a lid, sterilised

In a dry frying pan gently toast the coriander, cumin and caraway seeds until they are a shade darker and aromatic. Use a pestle and mortar or coffee grinder to pound or blitz until finely ground. Set aside.

In the same pan, heat 1 tablespoon of the olive oil and gently fry the onion and chilli for about 10 minutes, until soft. Add the garlic and fry for another 1–2 minutes, until aromatic.

Transfer all the remaining ingredients together with the onion mix, remaining olive oil and spices to a food processor and blitz until smooth. Season with salt and pepper to taste.

thyme and rosemary salmoriglio

makes about 80ml

Salmoriglio is a pungent Italian herb oil, traditionally made with oregano or marjoram, but really good with thyme and rosemary too. It transforms dishes from perfectly good to 'What on earth is that, I MUST have the recipe?'!

10g rosemary leaves

10g thyme leaves

¼ tsp sea salt

1 garlic clove

squeeze of lemon juice

4 tbsp extra virgin olive oil

Put the herbs in a mortar with the salt and the garlic. Pound relentlessly with a pestle until you have a smooth paste. Add a squeeze of lemon juice and slowly pour in the olive oil, stirring as you go with the pestle until everything is combined. It should be stored in the fridge, covered, and keeps for about 3 days.

labneh

**makes about
350–400g**

This Middle Eastern strained yoghurt is so easy to
make and is delicious on toasted sourdough, or as
a base for sandwiches and roasted vegetables (see
sourdough French toast, page 160, and bruschetta,
page 146). It is also wonderful with fruit, but if you
want to serve it with something sweet, reduce the
salt quantity to ¼ teaspoon and then drizzle over a
little maple syrup. I have made it successfully with soy
yoghurt too, so there is no need to miss out on the fun
if you are vegan. One of my favourite ways of serving
labneh is with a mixture of chopped tomatoes, olives,
parsley and sumac, and the best extra virgin olive oil
you can find. Then mop it all up with chunks of warm
spelt sourdough.

**500g full-fat Greek
or soy yoghurt**

¾ tsp fine sea salt

In a bowl, combine the yoghurt and salt and line
another bowl with a piece of muslin. Pour in the
yoghurt mixture and secure the muslin around the
yoghurt with an elastic band and suspend it over a
deep bowl – I find the handle of a wooden spoon
handy for this. Refrigerate for at least 24 hours, and
up to 2 days. The longer you leave it the more liquid
will drain off and the thicker the yoghurt will become.
Transfer to an airtight container and store in the fridge
for up to 1 week, or devour immediately as suggested
in the introduction.

tahini three ways

I: tahini verde

makes 250g

The vinegar-and-Dijon hit from a good salsa verde is anchored here by the earthy tahini: it's just delicious. If you ever have any lacklustre vegetables and are wondering how to bring them back to life, just blanch them in salted water and cover them in this stuff. For a cumin tahini variation, see whole baked cauliflower with cumin tahini, page 130.

Handful flat-leaf parsley leaves

Handful mint leaves

Handful basil leaves

2 cloves garlic, crushed

1 tsp Dijon mustard

1 tbsp red wine vinegar

6 tbsp tahini

4 tbsp extra virgin olive oil

1 tbsp capers, rinsed and drained, roughly chopped

Pinch of sea salt

75ml water

Put all the ingredients into the bowl of a food processor together with the water. Blitz until smooth. Taste and adjust the seasoning if necessary.

2: doenjang or miso tahini

makes about 200g

Doenjang, the Korean fermented soya bean paste, is a match made in heaven with creamy tahini. As is its Japanese counterpart, miso, or Korea's fiery paste, gochujang. These sauces can be used in any kind of salad, or as a dip. You can make it as thick or as thin as you like; just adjust the quantity of water in the recipe.

4 tbsp tahini

1½ tbsp doenjang
or miso paste

1 tbsp lemon juice

1 garlic clove, crushed

4–6 tbsp warm water

pinch of sea salt
and pepper

Put all the ingredients in a bowl and whisk vigorously until thoroughly combined. Taste and adjust the seasoning if necessary.

3: gochujang tahini

Follow the above recipe, substituting 1 tablespoon gochujang for the doenjang.

garlic confit

makes 2 x
250g jars

This recipe has two uses: the slow-baked mellow garlic can be served whole or crushed into any number of dips and dressings, and the perfumed oil that the garlic was cooked in can be used for frying and seasoning as well. It is really easy to make, keeps well and packs in mountains of flavour. What's not to love? As you are cooking the oil, regular olive oil is fine here.

6 garlic heads, cloves
separated and peeled

400ml olive oil

2 sprigs of rosemary

2 sprigs of thyme

2 x 250g glass jar
with a lid, sterilised

Preheat the oven to 180°C/160°C fan/Gas mark 4.

Put all the ingredients into a small baking dish, ensuring that the garlic cloves are fully submerged in the olive oil. Cover completely with foil and bake for 40–45 minutes, until the garlic is soft and golden.

Remove from the oven and leave to cool completely. Transfer to jars and store in the fridge for up to 1 month.

lemon confit

If you are looking for a similar kind of thing to preserved lemons, but without the one-month wait, then this is ideal. It can be used in all the same ways: chopped into salads, sauces, yoghurts, grains and so on. The oil, lemon juice and garlic are equally useful additions to dressings and sauces.

4 unwaxed lemons

100ml olive oil

1 garlic clove

2 sprigs of rosemary

pinch of sea salt

500ml airtight container, sterilised

Slice 2 lemons crossways into round discs, as thinly as possible. Bring a small saucepan of water to a rolling boil and blanch the lemon discs for 30 seconds. Remove the lemon discs, discard the water, then bring another saucepan of water to the boil and blanch for 30 seconds again. Repeat this process 1 more time, 3 times in total. Having a full kettle on the boil throughout this process speeds things up dramatically!

Juice the remaining 2 lemons, and put the juice in a saucepan together with the olive oil, garlic, rosemary and salt. Add the blanched lemon discs and set over a low heat. Simmer gently for 12–15 minutes, then remove from the heat and leave to cool completely. Transfer to an airtight container and top up with more oil if necessary to keep the lemons submerged. Store in the fridge for up to 1 month.

baked chilli oil

makes 500ml

Nancy, a great friend of ours from LA, brought us three full shopping bags of the most wonderful-smelling dried Mexican chillies on her most recent trip to London. I hadn't a notion of what I would do with such an enormous quantity, but Nancy came to the rescue with a whole range of ideas. One of them was this divine chilli oil that can be used to flavour anything and everything. I made it with the ancho, guajillo and mulato chillies that she gave us, but you can also make a delicious version with dried chipotle chillies, which are readily available on this side of the pond.

12 dried chillies of your choice

500ml olive oil

2 sprigs of rosemary

2 sprigs of thyme

500ml airtight container, sterilised

Preheat the oven to 160°C/140°C fan/Gas mark 3.

Put all the ingredients in a baking dish, ensuring that the chillies are fully submerged in the olive oil. Cover completely with foil and bake for 2 hours. Remove and leave to cool completely.

Strain off the oil through a sieve, and store the oil in an airtight container in the fridge for up to 6 months.

baked tomatoes in a spiced oil

**makes about
1 litre**

There is nothing that is not improved by a spoonful or two of these slow-baked tomatoes in olive oil. I tend to make a massive quantity, as I go through the stuff at an alarming rate, so feel free to double the recipe if you wish. It is delicious dolloped on to labneh with bread, mixed into salads, spooned over roast vegetables or added to a tomato sauce towards the end of preparation.

800g very ripe baby
plum tomatoes

2 sprigs of rosemary

5 garlic cloves, halved

2 tsp cumin seeds

2 tsp coriander seeds

1.5 tsp sea salt

750ml olive oil, plus
more to top up

4 x 250ml glass jar with
a lid, sterilised

Preheat the oven to 150°C/130°C fan/Gas mark 2.

Put all the ingredients in a small baking dish. Cover completely with foil and bake for 1½ hours. Remove the foil and continue to cook for another 30 minutes.

Remove from the oven and leave to cool completely. Transfer the tomatoes to jars, and if necessary top up with oil to cover. Store in the fridge for 2–3 weeks.

garlic and herb oils

makes about 80ml

These can be made at the very last moment and added to cooked grains and pulses, or served as a sauce over roasted vegetables, or fish or meat. Once made, they keep for a few days in the fridge in an airtight container.

20g fresh herbs (basil, flat-leaf parsley, mint, coriander, rosemary, thyme, etc.)

¼ tsp sea salt

1 garlic clove, crushed

extra virgin olive oil

airtight container
if storing, sterilised

Finely chop the herbs you are using. Put it in a bowl with the salt and crushed garlic. Slowly pour in 4 tablespoons of the olive oil, stirring as you go, until everything is well combined.

If you are using a woody herb like thyme or rosemary, discard the stalks and bash the leaves, garlic and salt into a paste using a pestle and mortar, then slowly trickle in the oil, stirring all the time until well combined.

yoghurt three ways

This is another easy way to jazz up any salad or roast vegetable dish. These can be made in advance too, allowing all the flavours to get to know one another.

garlic yoghurt

6 cloves garlic, skins left on

1 tsp olive oil

300ml Greek or soy yoghurt

Pinch sea salt

cumin yoghurt

3 tsp cumin seeds

1 tsp olive oil

300ml Greek or soy yoghurt

Pinch sea salt

mint yoghurt

Handful mint, finely chopped

1 tsp olive oil

300ml Greek or soy yoghurt

Pinch sea salt

for the garlic yoghurt:

Preheat the oven to 200°C/180°C fan/Gas mark 6.

Toss the garlic cloves in the oil and roast for 20 minutes, until softened. Squeeze the cloves out of their skins, mash with a fork and combine with the yoghurt and salt.

for the cumin yoghurt:

Put the cumin seeds in a dry frying pan and set over a medium heat. Pan fry for a few minutes, until aromatic. Put the seeds in a pestle and mortar and roughly bash to release the flavour. Follow the method for the garlic yoghurt, then add the bashed-up cumin seeds.

for the mint yoghurt:

Follow the method for the garlic yoghurt, then add the chopped mint.

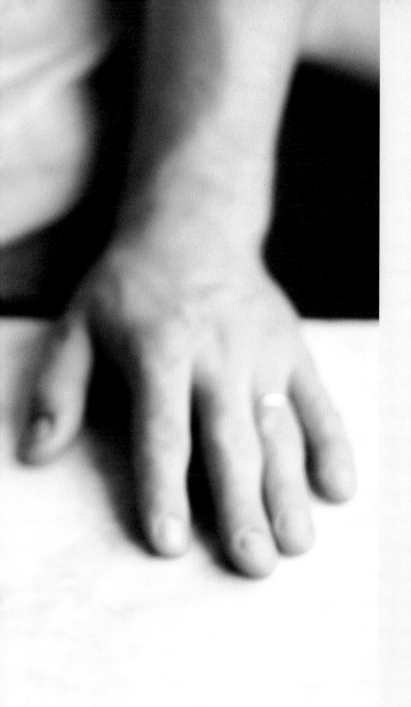

ferments and pickles

Making ferments and pickles could not be simpler. Yes, it requires a bit of patience, but the incredible flavour and health benefits will be your reward. Try not to think about it too much, just throw yourself in by making a few jars. They will be ready to eat within a month, and not long after that you will be hooked. You can then make another batch so it is ready by the time you have finished the first few jars. Ferments and pickles can be used in the same way as raw vegetables – they are extremely versatile, ready to be thrown into a salad, served as a snack with dips or layered into sandwiches.

fermentation

I am passionate about fermentation – it is an incredibly easy way to preserve vegetables and absolutely anyone can do it at home. All it involves is putting vegetables into a sterilised jar with salt and water, pressing down to get rid of any air pockets – and that's it. Yes, really! I have included plenty of information about its health benefits and some tips on how to use ferments below – not because it's complicated, but purely for your interest.

The myriad health benefits are a major incentive to making your own ferments, but the complex and ever-changing flavour profile is just as exciting – adding incredible bursts of flavour to salads, sandwiches, dressings or used just as a simple side dish to go with a main meal. Fermentation has been used as a form of traditional preservation in all food cultures at one time or another; it is only since refrigeration became commonplace that its popularity began to wane. Of course there are still many parts of the world where it is still common practice; Korea perhaps the country most famous for its love affair with all things fermented – with kimchi being the kingpin. However, we shouldn't forget that many of our most loved foods and drinks have gone through some form of fermentation – wine, beer, chocolate, cheese, coffee, yoghurt, sourdough bread and miso paste are just some of the fermented foods we consume on a daily basis.

so what exactly is fermentation?

When we talk about vegetable fermentation, the process is known as lacto fermentation – with the 'lacto' referring to the healthy bacteria, 'lactobacillus', which is present on the skin of every vegetable, and is all around us, even on our own bodies. When sliced vegetables are soaked in a salt-water liquid, or better still their own brine, created when salt is sprinkled over them, this process of lacto-fermentation begins. It allows the growth of the bacteria lactobacillus, which breaks down and eats the sugars present in the vegetables, converting them into lactic acid. This lactic acid is what gives fermented vegetables their characteristically tart/sour flavour. It also acts as a natural preservative, inhibiting the growth of harmful bacteria and increasing or preserving the vitamin and enzyme levels, as well as making vegetables more easy to digest.

why are fermented vegetables good for us?

Fermented vegetables are low in sugar but rich in fibre, minerals, nutrients and amino acids, and contain up to a thousand times more lactobacillus than yoghurt. The live bacteria, or probiotics, contained in fermented foods are great for our digestive tracts, helping to restore the natural balance of healthy gut bacteria, which have diminished over time from our use of antibiotic drugs and chlorinated water.

what to do with the ferments?

The same thing you would do with any raw vegetable. I love to chop them up into salads, or keep them in larger chunks or slices and eat them as a snack with hummus. I don't use them in cooking, as the heat would kill off the majority of the good bacteria, vitamins and minerals.

use the best ingredients you can

Vegetable ferments consist of nothing more than the vegetable itself, salt and water, and perhaps a few seasoning ingredients – so it is important that you use the best-quality ingredients you can afford. I would recommend organic vegetables, good-quality sea salt or Himalayan rock salt and filtered water to ensure the best quality. Also bear in mind that you should avoid using any metal utensils/storage containers – the salt and acids in the ferment will corrode them.

salt-water brine mixture

Some vegetables, like courgettes and cabbages, can produce enough water to create their own brine when they have been grated and salted. Other firmer vegetables, like carrots and parsnips, or vegetables that have been cut into slices rather than being grated, usually need some extra salt-water mixture added to them, to ensure that they are fully submerged. The brine should taste saltier than you want your vegetable ferment to taste, and some firmer vegetables, especially those that have been cut into thicker slices, can take a bit more salt. The brines will usually contain 1–2 tablespoons of salt per 500ml of water. Also bear in mind that vegetables will soak up some of the liquid in the initial stage of the ferment, and you will therefore need to keep them topped up so they stay submerged. My top-up solution is roughly 1 tablespoon of salt per 500ml of water.

to grate or to slice?

If you choose to grate, there is a higher chance that the vegetable will produce enough of its own brine to submerge it once it has been salted. If you slice, you are more likely to need to make your own salt water solution to top up the brine. Either works well. To top up the brine, dissolve 1 tablespoon of sea salt per 500ml water.

what vegetables can I ferment?

You can ferment any vegetable, but do bear in mind that with something like beetroot, there is a higher quantity of sugar present, which can convert to alcohol quite easily, so it is better to mix it with another less sweet vegetable – like a leafy green.

how do I sterilise my jars?

I find the quickest way to sterilise jars is to put them into an oven preheated to 180°C/160°C fan/Gas mark 4 for 5 minutes. Make sure you set a timer, as any longer may result in the glass cracking. Any rubber seals should be removed before sterilising.

at what temperature should I be storing my ferments?

The rate of fermentation will depend on the temperature and environment in which the ferment is being stored. Between 15°C and 18°C (out of direct sunlight) will produce a good ferment in around one to four weeks, at which point you can transfer it to the fridge. However, the precise point at which you transfer the ferment to the fridge is a matter of personal preference, so it is important to taste the ferment regularly after a few days or a week at room temperature, and once you are happy with the degree of sourness and complexity of flavour, transfer it to the fridge. Once it is refrigerated, the rate of fermentation will slow down dramatically, so this enables you to maintain a flavour profile that you are happy with – although even in the fridge the flavours will still continue to develop and become more complex. Low-and-slow ferments tend to produce more nuanced flavours. If you live in a hot climate (or are making ferments in the summertime) things really do speed up dramatically and you will notice they begin to fizz and bubble within just a few days, so keep a close eye on them, taste regularly and move them to the fridge when you are happy with the flavour profile. Once in the fridge you can always take them out again for a day or two if you want to develop the flavour even further.

burping your ferments

Don't be alarmed! If you are using an air-tight lid it is common for there to be a build-up of gas at room temperature. To avoid this, simply open your jar once a day to let any gas escape, then reseal and continue as normal.

keeping the vegetables submerged with weights

If necessary, you can use a weight to keep the vegetables in place if they begin to float. My weight of choice is a small, flat, clean stone wrapped in a cabbage leaf or greaseproof paper.

how do I know if my ferment has gone bad?

The key to success with vegetable ferments is ensuring that the vegetables are completely submerged in the brine at all times, so be sure to top up the ferment with extra home-made brine if necessary, and use weights to keep the vegetables submerged if they float. The ferment should smell tangy and sour, but still pleasant, and it will often be a bit fizzy – this is quite normal. If, however, there is a foul smell or you notice mould developing deep inside the jar, you should discard it. A small amount of mould on the rim of the jar is usually fine, as long as the vegetables are submerged – just wipe it away with a clean cloth. As ever, a degree of common sense is necessary here. Trust your instincts, but take comfort in the knowledge that it is very rare for ferments to go bad if the vegetables have been handled properly and are fully submerged in the brine with no air pockets, as they are preserved by the lactic acid.

rainbow radish ferment

makes 750ml jar

I always seem to have an extra bunch of radishes lying around the fridge in the spring and summer, no matter how much I plan. So I ended up fermenting a bunch one day, and now I think I prefer them that way.

500ml water

1½ tbsp sea salt

450g radishes, any variety you like – breakfast radishes, the coloured ones, etc.

¼ tsp caraway seeds

1 x 750ml jar with a lid, sterilised

Combine the water and salt until the salt is fully dissolved. Wash the radishes, top and tail them, and cut them into ½ cm slices.

Put the caraway seeds into the base of your sterilised jar. Add the radish and pour over the brine to about 2cm below the rim, so that everything is fully submerged. If necessary, use a weight to keep the radishes submerged, then seal the jar with a lid and ferment for 4–10 days at room temperature (see the notes on page 234), tasting after about 2 days. Once you are happy with the level of fermentation achieved, store the jar in the fridge, where it will keep for months.

parsnip and chilli ferment

makes 750ml jar

Parsnips have a subtle sweetness that I love, and this vegetable works really well as a ferment. You could use carrots here too. I love it chopped into salads, or just as a snack with hummus. The chillies can be eaten too, and they only provide a subtle heat to the brine, but they can be replaced with whole cloves of garlic if you are averse to any kind of chilli kick.

450g parsnips, peeled, and ends removed

1 red chilli

1 green chilli

½ tsp chilli flakes (or Korean chilli powder, gochugaru)

1 tbsp sea salt

500ml water

1 x 750ml jar with a lid, sterilised

Cut the parsnips in half lengthways and then into 1cm-thick lengths. Try them out in the sterilised jar you will be using; ideally they should be about 2cm shorter than the full height of the jar. Halve the chillies and remove the seeds.

Put the chilli flakes in the sterilised jar. In a jug, dissolve the salt in the water, stirring to combine. Tightly pack all the parsnips and chillies into the jar, then pour over the brine to about 2cm below the rim, so that the vegetables are fully submerged.

If necessary, use a weight to keep the vegetables down, then seal the jar with a lid and ferment for 5–10 days at room temperature (see the notes on page 234), tasting after about 4 days. Once you are happy with the level of fermentation achieved, store the jar in the fridge, where it will keep for months.

fermented garlic

**makes 1 x
500ml jar**

Fermenting mellows out the sharper, more pungent notes of raw garlic, giving it a unique and delicious flavour. This can then be used in exactly the same way you would use regular garlic, with the added bonus of the cloves being ready peeled. Cooking the garlic cloves does negate a lot of the beneficial aspects of the ferment, so I tend to use them raw in salads, dressings and so on. If you find raw garlic too much to handle, this is certainly worth a try.

500ml water

1 tbsp sea salt

10–12 garlic heads, cloves removed and peeled

1 tsp dried oregano

1 x 500ml jar with a lid, sterilised

Combine the water and salt until the salt is fully dissolved.

Pack the garlic cloves into the jar, together with the dried oregano. Pour over the brine to about 2cm below the rim, so that everything is fully submerged.

If necessary, use a weight to keep everything down, then seal the jar with a lid and ferment for 3–4 weeks at room temperature (see the notes on page 234), tasting after about 2 weeks – garlic does tend to need longer than most other vegetables to get going. Once you are happy with the level of fermentation achieved, store the jar in the fridge, where it will keep for months (up to 1 year), with the flavour profile mellowing further and becoming more and more delicious.

carrot, apple and ginger pickle

I made this pickle one day after making a carrot and apple juice. I had some carrots and apples left over, so I popped them in a jar with this easy sweet and sour pickling liquid. This is delicious sliced into a salad.

300ml apple cider or rice vinegar

300ml filtered water

180ml clear honey

1 tsp sea salt

4 bay leaves

4 juniper berries

250g organic carrots, peeled and cut into thin slices lengthways, to fit your jar

75g organic apples, cored and cut into thin slices

25g fresh ginger, peeled and cut into thin slices

1 x 750ml jar with a lid, sterilised

Put the vinegar, water, honey, salt, bay leaves and juniper berries in a pot and bring them to the boil. The moment it begins to boil, reduce the heat to low and simmer gently for 5 minutes. Remove from the heat and leave to cool completely.

Place the carrot, apple and ginger in the sterilised jar and pour over the cold liquid to about 1cm below the rim of the jar, so that everything is submerged. Seal with a lid and store in a cool dark place for about 3 weeks, or longer. Once opened, store in the fridge and consume within 1 month.

sauerkraut

**makes 1 x
1-litre jar**

This is arguably the most well-known ferment in the world, or at least on a par with kimchi, but it is often mistaken for a pickle. In fact there is no vinegar used at all; a traditional kraut will contain nothing more than cabbage and salt, with perhaps a spice added in, as I have done here. This is a great place to start if you are new to the fermenting world, and feel free to play around with this – you can use red cabbage, or make a kale kraut, add in other spices, or other grated vegetables.

**1 large head white
cabbage (about 1kg)**

1–1½ tbsp sea salt

**1 tsp fennel seeds,
or other spice**

**1 x 1-litre jar with
a lid, sterilised**

Remove the outer leaves of the cabbage, then finely shred it – a mandolin is very handy for this. Transfer the cabbage to a bowl and sprinkle over the salt, using a little more or less depending on the weight of your cabbage. At this stage it should taste a bit saltier than you want it to once it has fermented.

Vigorously massage the salt into the cabbage for 10–15 minutes. Use the blunt end of a rolling pin to bash the cabbage as you go, which helps to release the juices. Keep going until the cabbage has released a good amount of liquid – the more the better, as the aim is to completely submerge the cabbage in its own brine. Add the fennel seeds, and stir to combine.

Begin layering the cabbage and its juice into a sterilised jar a little at a time, pressing it very firmly down as you go, until you are about 2–3cm below the lid. It is imperative that the cabbage is completely submerged and there are no air pockets. If you have not managed to extract enough juice from the cabbage to submerge it, combine 250ml of water and 1½ teaspoons of salt until dissolved, and use this to top up the jar. Giving the jar a light bang on your work surface will also help to bring any air bubbles up to the surface.

ferments and pickles

Once you are confident that the cabbage is covered in brine and none of it is sticking up above the surface, seal the jar. If necessary, use a weight to keep everything down, then seal the jar and ferment for about 2 weeks at room temperature (depending on the temperature of your home; see the notes on page 234), tasting it after about 10 days.

Once you are happy with the level of fermentation achieved, store the jar in the fridge, where it will keep for months.

cabbage and kale kimchi

makes 1 x
1-litre jar

1 large Napa/Chinese cabbage (roughly 1.2kg)

150g kale, stalks removed (I find cavolo nero works best)

1.2l of water

40g fine table salt

60g sea salt

flour paste

1½ tbsp glutinous rice flour, or plain flour

230ml water

paste

7 garlic cloves

5g fresh root ginger, peeled

100g onion, peeled

50g goghugaru (Korean chilli powder)

80ml fish sauce

2 tsp soy sauce

1 tbsp coconut palm sugar or maple syrup

2 tbsp rice vinegar

This is a take on authentic Korean cabbage kimchi. Traditionally it is made with Napa or Chinese cabbage, but the addition of kale also works really well, and it lends its own particular flavour and texture. In Korea, fermented baby prawns are also added to the seasoning mix to give it a more robust flavour that Koreans adore, but it is not crucial to the making of good kimchi, so I have left it out here. If you don't want your kimchi quite as spicy, you can reduce the gochugaru chilli powder a little. As time goes by, kimchi gets progressively more sour, at which point it is delicious pan-fried with sesame oil and a tiny bit of honey. Try it out in the kimchi, egg and avocado on sourdough recipe on page 144.

Cut about 10cm deep across the base of the cabbage, then gently split the entire cabbage in half lengthways. Rinse the cabbage and kale under running water, getting in between the leaves. In a large flat bowl or container, combine the 1.2 litres of water with the 40g table salt. Sprinkle the 60g of sea salt over each leaf of the halved cabbage, focusing your attention on the thicker root end and working up to the thinner leaf. Put any remaining salt into the salt-water mixture. Place the cabbage cut side down in the bowl of salted water and mix the kale in around it. Press firmly down on the cabbage and kale to help the leaves soak up the salt water. It will not be submerged, though. Leave to soak for 2 hours, then turn over and soak for a further 2 hours, until the cabbage leaves are limp and bend easily without breaking. Make sure to time this process so you don't over-salt the cabbage.

vegetables

200g carrots, peeled and cut into fine julienne strips

30g chives, cut into 4cm lengths

4 spring onions, halved lengthways and cut into 4cm lengths

1 x 1-litre jar with a lid, sterilised

Drain the cabbage and kale and rinse thoroughly under running water at least twice. Taste the leaves: they should be highly salted; however, if it is too strong, keep rinsing until the salt levels are reduced, then drain completely.

In the meantime, mix the glutinous rice flour with 2 tablespoons of the water, using a fork or whisk to ensure there are no lumps. Once you have a smooth paste, gradually pour the remaining water into the flour mixture. Put the mixture into a saucepan, bring to the boil stirring all the time, then reduce the heat to low and simmer gently for 5 minutes, until thick and gelatinous. Remove from the heat and leave to cool completely.

In a food processor, combine all the paste ingredients and the cooled flour mixture, until you have a smooth paste. Add this to a bowl, together with the carrot, chives and spring onions, and mix well until thoroughly combined. Carefully apply this mixture to the drained cabbage, layering the leaves of kale into the cabbage as you go, ensuring every leaf is covered with the mixture. Use the outer leaf of each half to wrap around the cabbage, helping to keep the mixture secure inside.

Put the cabbage into a sterilised jar or other airtight container, press down firmly to remove any air pockets and seal tightly. Keep the jar at room temperature (out of direct sunlight) for 2 days, by which stage it should be beginning to ferment and smell a little sour. The rate of fermentation will depend on the temperature and climate of the location where you are making it, so a good way to gauge its progress is to taste it at this point – if it has developed those characteristically sour notes, then you are on the right track. Now use a spoon to press the kimchi down very firmly, submerging it in its own juices and making sure there are no air pockets at all. If you need to, place a smaller jar filled with water, or a small stone wrapped in greaseproof paper, on top of the cabbage to make sure it remains fully submerged. Seal the container again and refrigerate. Most people find they like the kimchi best after a few weeks in the fridge; others like it after a month or 2, when it has a bit more of a sour kick to it. Try it out at intervals and see when you like it best. If kept in a very cold fridge, it will keep for about a year.

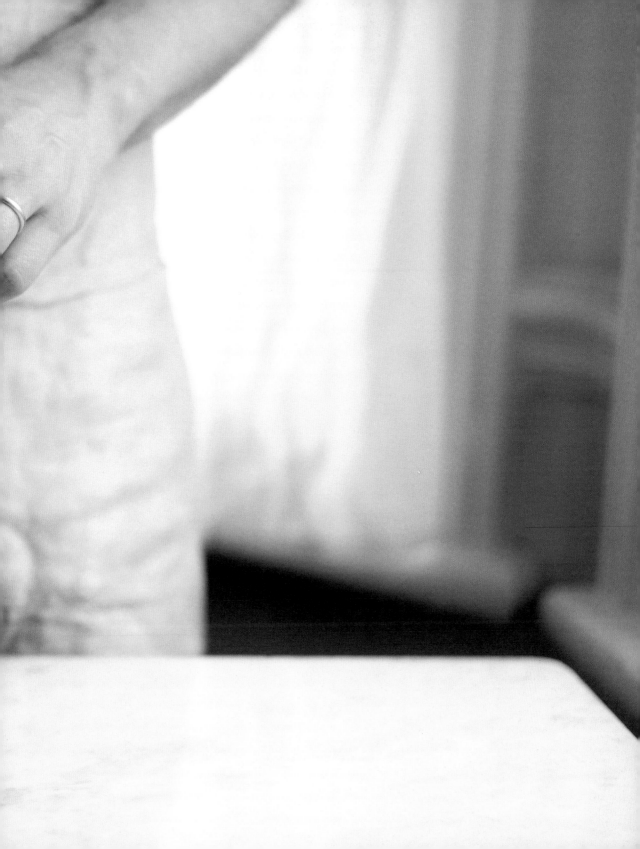

cucumber ferment

makes 1 x
1-litre jar

These are more commonly known as kosher dill
pickles, because they were popularised in New York's
kosher Jewish delis, where they pack their ferments
with dill and garlic. I find the name a bit misleading,
though, as it is not a pickle at all . . . so cucumber
ferment it is! Also, if you are not a fan of dill you can
just leave it out.

3 tbsp sea salt

1 litre water

5 garlic cloves

4 black peppercorns

1 tsp mustard seeds

5–6 pickling or
Persian cucumbers

8–10 sprigs of fresh dill

1 x 1-litre jar with
a lid, sterilised

Combine the salt and water until the salt is fully
dissolved. Peel the garlic cloves and slice in
half lengthways.

Place half the garlic in the base of the sterilised jar,
together with all the peppercorns and mustard seeds.
Tightly pack in the cucumbers, dill and remaining
garlic, then pour over the brine to about 2cm below
the rim, so that everything is fully submerged.

If you need to, use a weight to keep everything down,
then seal the jar with a lid and ferment for 3–8 days
at room temperature (see the notes on page 234),
tasting after about 2 days. The brine will eventually
become slightly fizzy, and the cucumbers will be sour.
Once you are happy with the level of fermentation
achieved, store the jar in the fridge, where it will
keep for months.

pickled seaweed sauce

makes 1 litre

My Korean wife and mother-in-law make all sorts of pickles and preserves, and they were my original inspiration for this time-honoured method of food preservation. There is no doubt that some ferments and pickles take a very long time to mature, particularly in this case, but I really believe they are worth the investment. What you lose in time you gain in flavour. It is simply impossible to create the same unique and nuanced flavour profiles in any other way. It takes about 2 minutes to make this concoction, so just do it. Put it in a dark corner somewhere and forget about it. Three to six months later, you will have your reward. My main use for this is salad dressings – just combine one part of the pickle liquid with two parts extra virgin olive oil, and balance it out with a little more vinegar and mustard. In Korea, it is combined with soy sauce as a dip for tofu and dumplings, which is also delicious drizzled over salads.

500ml brown rice vinegar

500ml honey

40g kombu seaweed

1 x 1-litre jar with a lid, sterilised

Combine the vinegar and honey and pour them into a 1-litre sterilised resealable glass jar. Cut the kombu into pieces that will easily fit into the neck of the jar. Add the kombu to the liquid, ensuring the pieces are completely submerged.

Leave the jar in a cool, dark spot for a minimum of 3 months, but ideally 6, and use as described in the introduction. If stored correctly, these will keep forever.

cauliflower, dried chilli and mustard seed pickle

makes 750ml jar

I enjoy this cauliflower pickle as a simple snack with good bread and extra virgin olive oil, or mixed into salads. You can up the quantity of chilli if you like a bit more heat.

300ml apple cider vinegar

300ml filtered water

90ml clear honey

1 tsp sea salt

2 tsp mustard seeds

1 tsp dried chilli

450g cauliflower, cut into small florets

1 x 750ml jar with a lid, sterilised

Put the vinegar, water, honey, salt, mustard seeds and dried chilli into a saucepan and bring them to the boil. The moment it begins to boil, reduce the heat to low and simmer gently for 5 minutes. Remove from the heat and leave to cool completely.

Put the cauliflower into the sterilised jar and pour over the cold liquid to about 1cm below the rim of the jar, so that everything is submerged. Seal with a lid and store in a cool, dark place for 3–4 weeks before opening. It will keep for about 8–10 months like this, but once opened, keep refrigerated and consume within 1 month.

fennel and dill pickle

makes 750ml jar

This is particularly good added to fresh coleslaw – or, for a delicious crunch, add it to a sandwich or salad.

300ml apple
cider vinegar

300ml filtered water

180ml clear honey

1 tsp sea salt

2 juniper berries

1 allspice berry

3 large fennel bulbs

4 sprigs of fresh dill

1 x 750ml jar with a lid,
sterilised

Put the vinegar, water, honey, salt, juniper berries and allspice into a pot and bring to the boil. The moment it begins to boil, reduce the heat to low and simmer gently for 5 minutes. Remove from the heat and leave to cool completely.

Remove the tough outer layers of the fennel bulbs, and slice very thinly – a mandolin is useful for this. Place the fennel into the sterilised jar together with the dill, and pour over the cold liquid to about 1cm below the rim of the jar, so that everything is submerged. Seal with a lid and store in a cool, dark place for 2–3 weeks before opening. It will keep for about 6 months like this, but once opened keep refrigerated and consume within 1 month.

quick pickled onions

makes 750ml jar

Unlike the other pickles, this can be eaten within hours of being made, although a day or two is ideal. The onions are delicious as a topping for the smørrebrød, page 156, or the Buddha bowl, page 180.

180ml red wine vinegar

350ml filtered water

3 tbsp clear honey

1 tsp sea salt

1 tsp cumin seeds

500g red onions, halved and thinly sliced

1 x 750ml jar with a lid, sterilised

Put the vinegar, water, honey, salt and cumin seeds into a saucepan and bring to the boil. The moment it begins to boil, reduce the heat to low and simmer gently for 5 minutes. Remove from the heat and leave to cool completely.

Put the red onion into the jar and pour over the cold liquid to about 1cm below the rim of the jar, so that everything is submerged. Seal with a lid and store in a cool, dark place for 1–2 days before opening. It will keep for about 3 months like this, but once opened, keep refrigerated and consume within 3–4 weeks.

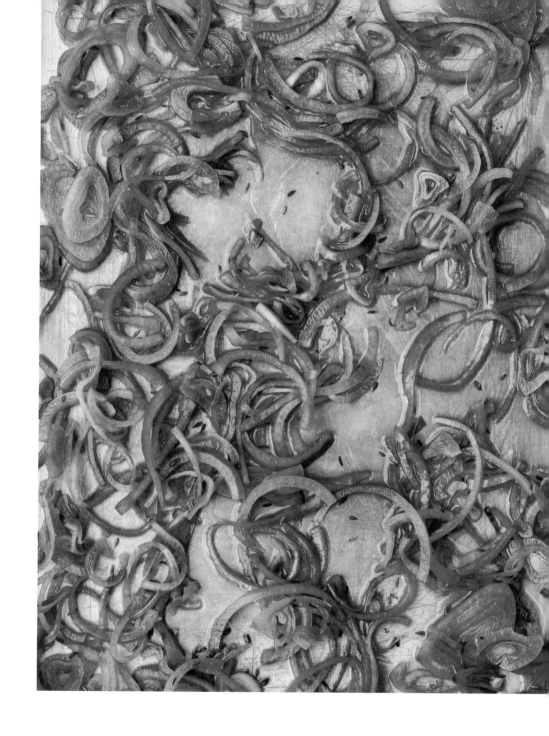

korean pickled fruit in soju and honey

makes 1 x
1.5-litre jar

Lining the shelves above my mother-in-law's sink in Seoul, South Korea, are a number of weird and wonderful-looking jars. The most beautiful are a row of fruit-filled jars; the plump skin of the fruits ever so slightly dulled with time, suspended in a mixture of soju, the ubiquitous Korean rice liquor, honey and rice vinegar. These jars of preserved fruit have two uses. First, the sweet perfumed liquid is used in combination with vinegar and soy sauce to create a dipping sauce for Korean dishes that will blow your mind, it is so delicious. Second, the fruit itself is served up in small portions as a side dish, offering a little sweetness alongside robustly flavoured Korean hotpots. In a more Western context, the fruit is sublime with yoghurt and granola, or squished on to toasted bread as a kind of jam, and the sweet liquor is delicious in salad dressings, or indeed in your cocktail of choice.

500g stone fruit of
your choice

400ml clear honey

150ml rice wine vinegar

300ml soju, sake or
200ml vodka and
100ml water

1 cinnamon stick

1 star anise (optional)

1 x 1.5-litre jar with
a lid, sterilised

Wash the fruit, halve them and remove the stones.

Put the rest of the ingredients into a saucepan and bring them to the boil, then remove them from the heat and leave to cool.

Put the fruit into a sterilised jar, and cover with the cold liquid up to about 2cm below the rim, so the fruit is fully submerged. Cover and leave to marinate in a cool dark spot or in the fridge for at least 2 months (ideally up to half a year) before eating. The perfect time to make these jars is in the summer when you have a glut of stone fruit at your fingertips. They will then be perfectly muddled in their marinade when Christmas rolls around – the ideal time to sample sweet fruit and perfumed liquor.

soy pickled eggs

makes 6

There is no denying that this is not the most attractive dish – but the eggs taste great, so who cares? This is a Korean side dish, where boiled eggs are simmered in a soy sauce stock that permeates the whites of the eggs, giving them a delicious flavour. Once cool they can be eaten as a snack, as they do in Korea, or sliced into salads.

Water, for boiling

2 tsp salt

6 organic eggs

4 garlic cloves, peeled

150ml soy sauce

280ml water

2 tbsp honey

Bring a small saucepan of water and the salt to the boil, add the eggs and simmer for 8 minutes exactly. Drain and cool in ice-cold water.

Once they are cool, peel the eggs. Return them to the saucepan with the remaining ingredients and bring to the boil. Reduce the heat to low and simmer gently for 20 minutes, stirring the eggs frequently until they are a deep brown colour. Remove from the heat and leave to cool completely. Store in an airtight container in the fridge for up to 4 days.

herb vinegars

makes 1 x 500ml glass bottle

Making flavoured herb vinegars is as simple as combining the two ingredients together, and then they provide wonderful additional flavour. There are some key tips to remember though. First, avoid using any metal utensils or containers, as they will react with the vinegar. Also, make sure the acidity of the vinegar is at least 5 per cent (it will say it on the bottle), as this will ensure that the herbs are preserved. And finally, remember to top up your vinegar after using it, as the herbs must always remain submerged.

5 sprigs of fresh herbs (tarragon, rosemary, dill, thyme, marjoram, basil, etc.)

500ml organic white wine vinegar, plus extra to top up

1 x 500ml glass bottle. Narrow-neck glass bottles are handy for this, as this shape keeps the herbs from floating up above the surface of the vinegar.

Lightly bruise the herbs you are using. If they are tougher, woodier herbs like rosemary or thyme, you can gently bash them once or twice using a pestle and mortar or a rolling pin. If they are more delicate, like tarragon, lightly roll the herbs between the palms of your hands. Either way, the herbs should remain completely intact – you are just waking them up.

Gently tease the sprigs of herbs through the neck of the bottle. Use a plastic funnel to pour in the vinegar, making sure the herbs are completely submerged. Seal the bottle, and store in a cool, dark cupboard for 2 weeks before using. The longer you leave the vinegar, the stronger the infusion will become.

index

aioli baked leeks, almonds and aioli 134

allergies and intolerance 10

almond baked leeks, almonds and aioli 134

fig, almond and cinnamon sourdough 40

spanish bread and almond soup 155

amaranth 167

quick red lentil and amaranth dhal with courgette and tomato 184

apple carrot, apple and ginger pickle 242

wild rice, apple, tomato and teff salad 172

apricot apricot tartlets 90

buckwheat, hazelnut and dried apricot sourdough 38

aubergine aubergine caponata and labneh 146

balsamic baked aubergines, mushrooms and farro 132

avocado Buddha bowl with squash, ginger, cucumber, avocado and seaweed 180–1

kimchi, egg and avocado on sourdough 144

smashed chickpeas and avocado 147

sourdough french toast with avocado, tomato and labneh 160

baked chilli oil 222

baked leeks, almonds and aioli 134

baked oats with mango, blueberries and banana 195

baked sweet potato and beetroot with roasted freekeh and salmoriglio 136

baked tomatoes in a spiced oil 224

balsamic vinegar balsamic baked aubergines, mushrooms and farro 132

strawberry, balsamic and thyme jam 204

banana baked oats with mango, blueberries and banana 195

barley 166

pearl barley with smashed cucumber, pomegranate and walnuts 182

rye, barley and oat bircher muesli 194

basil roast fennel, squash, chorizo and basil frittata 118–19

beetroot baked sweet potato and beetroot with roasted freekeh and salmoriglio 136

beghrir pancakes with nectarines and honey 190–1

berry pie 102–4

black multigrain seed bread 52–3

black rice and coconut milk porridge 189

blackberry baked oats with mango, blueberries and banana 195

berry pie 102–4

blueberry berry pie 102–4

sourdough blueberry pancakes 44

bread 7, 13–40, 46–58, 64

equipment for making 15–16

notes on making 18–20

broad beans couscous with broad beans and pecans 175

bruschetta 146–7

buckwheat 167

buckwheat, hazelnut and dried apricot sourdough 38

plum and raspberry buckwheat crumble 106

buddha bowl with squash, ginger, cucumber, avocado and seaweed 180–1

bulgur wheat 166

cabbage and kale kimchi
246–7

cake gluten-free chocolate,
buckwheat and
cardamon 76

italian strawberry and
chocolate chunk 72

parsnip 74

peach, pistachio and
coconut 76

camargue red rice with
squash and cavolo nero
178

caramelised onion, sweet
potato and rye tart
124–5

cardamom gluten-free
chocolate, buckwheat
and cardamom cake
78–9

carrot carrot, apple and
ginger pickle 242

roasted carrots
with kamut, thyme,
hazelnuts and garlic
yoghurt 138

cauliflower cauliflower,
dried chilli and mustard
seed pickle 252

rye with cauliflower,
peaches and tahini 176

whole baked
cauliflower with cumin
tahini 130–1

cavolo nero camargue red
rice with squash and
cavolo nero 178

cheese Istanbul scrambled
egg sourdough with feta
and chorizo 142–3

strawberry, millet,
pistachios and goat's
cheese 170

cherry oat and cherry pie
94–5

chia oatcakes 66

chickpea smashed
chickpeas and avocado
147

chilli baked chilli oil 222

cauliflower, dried chilli
and mustard seed pickle
252

chilli tomato jam 208

chocolate chocolate,
cinnamon and pecan
babka 80–3

chocolate hazelnut tart
96–7

chocolate pastry 87

chocolate, tahini and
pecan rye cookies
108–9

gluten-free chocolate,
buckwheat and
cardamom cake 78–9

italian strawberry and
chocolate chunk cake
72–3

chorizo Istanbul scrambled
egg sourdough with feta
and chorizo 142–3

puy lentil and freekeh
soup with chorizo 186

roast fennel, squash,
chorizo and basil
frittata 118–19

cinnamon chocolate,
cinnamon and pecan
babka 80–3

fig, almond and
cinnamon sourdough
40

citrus curd of lemon and
orange 206

coconut, desiccated
coconut, tahini and
cranberry macaroons
110

peach, pistachio and
coconut cake 76

coconut cream hazelnut
coconut caramel tart
88–9

coconut milk black rice and
coconut milk porridge
189

coconut oil 11

coeliac 10

confit garlic 220

lemon 221

courgette quick red lentil
and amaranth dhal with
courgette and tomato
184

couscous 166

couscous with broad
beans and pecans 175

cranberry coconut,
tahini and cranberry
macaroons 110

cucumber buddha bowl
with squash, ginger,
cucumber, avocado and
seaweed 180–1

cucumber ferment 250

pearl barley with
smashed cucumber,
pomegranate and
walnuts 182

cumin yoghurt 228

date rye, pecan and date
loaf 50

dhal quick red lentil and
amaranth dhal with
courgette and tomato
184

dill fennel and dill pickle
254

doenjang 219

egg Istanbul scrambled egg sourdough with feta and chorizo 142–3

kimchi, egg and avocado on sourdough 144

soy pickled eggs 260

farinata with olives, red onion and rocket 120–1

farro 166

balsamic baked aubergines, mushrooms and farro 132

fennel fennel and dill pickle 254

roast fennel, squash, chorizo and basil frittata 118–19

fermentation 232–5

fermented garlic 240

feta Istanbul scrambled egg sourdough with feta and chorizo 142–3

fig fig, almond and cinnamon sourdough 40

fig and pistachio frangipane tart 92

freekeh 167

baked sweet potato and beetroot with roasted freekeh and salmoriglio 136

puy lentil and freekeh soup with chorizo 186

garlic fermented garlic 240

garlic and herb oils 226

garlic confit 220

garlic yoghurt 228

gazpacho 152

ginger buddha bowl with squash, ginger,

cucumber, avocado and seaweed 180–1

carrot, apple and ginger pickle 242

gluten 10

gluten-free chocolate, buckwheat and cardamom cake 78–9

gluten-free pastry 86

gluten-free sandwich loaf 58–9

gluten-free savoury pastry 123

goat's cheese strawberry, millet, pistachios and goat's cheese 170

grains soaking 168

sprouting 169

with wheat/gluten 166–7

without wheat/gluten 167

harissa 214

hazelnut buckwheat, hazelnut and dried apricot sourdough 38

chocolate hazelnut tart 96–7

hazelnut coconut caramel tart 88–9

roasted carrots with kamut, thyme, hazelnuts and garlic yoghurt 138

hemp seed spelt and hemp seed granola 196

herb vinegars 262

honey beghrir pancakes with nectarines and honey 190–1

korean pickled fruit in soju and honey 258

injera 42

istanbul scrambled egg sourdough with feta and chorizo 142–3

italian strawberry and chocolate chunk cake 72–3

jam chilli tomato 208

spiced raisin 202

strawberry, balsamic and thyme 204

kale cabbage and kale kimchi 246–7

kamut 166–7

roasted carrots with kamut, thyme, hazelnuts and garlic yoghurt 138

kimchi cabbage and kale kimchi 246–7

kimchi, egg and avocado on sourdough 144

kimchi salsa verde 212

kimchi sourdough 32

korean pickled fruit in soju and honey 258

labneh 216

aubergine caponata and labneh 146

sourdough french toast with avocado, tomato and labneh 160

leek baked leeks, almonds and aioli 134

lemon citrus curd of lemon and orange 206

lemon confit 221

preserved lemons 210

lentil puy lentil and freekeh soup with chorizo 186

quick red lentil and amaranth dhal with courgette and tomato 184

mackerel Turkish mackerel sourdough sandwich 150

mango baked oats with mango, blueberries and banana 195

maple rye and maple sourdough 36

marmalade rhubarb 200

millet 167

strawberry, millet, pistachios and goat's cheese 170

mint mint yoghurt 228

pea and mint purée 147

miso tahini 219

muesli rye, barley and oat bircher muesli 194

mushroom balsamic baked aubergines, mushrooms and farro 132

mushroom and farro soup 188

red onion, girolles and pine nut tart 128

mustard seed cauliflower, dried chilli and mustard seed pickle 252

nectarine beghrir pancakes with nectarines and honey 190–1

nuts, *see* hazelnuts, pine nuts, pistachio, walnuts

oats 167

baked oats with mango, blueberries and banana 195

oat and cherry pie 94–5

overnight sweet potato oats 192

olive aubergine caponata and labneh 146

farinata with olives, red onion and rocket 120–1

olive and herb yeasted bread 46–8

onion caramelised onion, sweet potato and rye tart 124–5

farinata with olives, red onion and rocket 120–1

pickled red onion 156

red onion, girolles and pine nut tart 128

orange citrus curd of lemon and orange 206

overnight sweet potato oats 192

pan con tomate 154

pancake beghrir with nectarines and honey 190

sourdough blueberry 44

panzanella salad 158

pappa al pomodoro soup 162–3

parsnip parsnip and chilli ferment 238

parsnip cake 74–5

pea and mint purée 147

peach apricot tartlets 90

peach, pistachio and coconut cake 76

rye with cauliflower, peaches and tahini 176

pear tarte Tatin 98–9

pearl barley with smashed cucumber, pomegranate and walnuts 182

pecan chocolate, cinnamon and pecan babka 80–3

chocolate, tahini and pecan rye cookies 108–9

couscous with broad beans and pecans 175

rye, pecan and date loaf 50

pickle carrot, apple and ginger 242

cauliflower, dried chilli and mustard seed 252

fennel and dill 254

korean pickled fruit in soju and honey 258

pickled red onion 156

pickled seaweed sauce 251

quick pickled onions 256

soy pickled eggs 260

pine nuts red onion, girolles and pine nut tart 128

pistachio fig and pistachio frangipane tart 92

peach, pistachio and coconut cake 76

strawberry, millet, pistachios and goat's cheese 170

pizetta 114–15

plum and raspberry buckwheat crumble 106

pomegranate pearl barley with smashed cucumber, pomegranate and walnuts 182

poppy spelt and poppy seed pitta 60–1

potatoes, new 156

preserved lemons 210

puy lentil and freekeh soup with chorizo 186

quick pickled onions 256

quick red lentil and amaranth dhal with courgette and tomato 184

radish rainbow radish ferment 236

rainbow radish ferment 236

raspberry plum and raspberry buckwheat crumble 106

red onion, girolles and pine nut tart 128

rhubarb marmalade 200–1

rice black rice and coconut milk porridge 189

camargue red rice with squash and cavolo nero 178

wild rice, apple, tomato and teff salad 172

roast fennel, squash, chorizo and basil frittata 118–19

roasted carrots with kamut, thyme, hazelnuts and garlic yoghurt 138

rocket farinata with olives, red onion and rocket 120–1

rosemary thyme and rosemary salmoriglio 215

rye 167

caramelised onion,

sweet potato and rye tart 124–5

rye, barley and oat bircher muesli 194

rye, pecan and date loaf 50

rye with cauliflower, peaches and tahini 176

spelt and rye pastry 123

super-fast, no-knead spelt and rye loaf 64

salad panzanella 158

wild rice, apple, tomato and teff 172

salmoriglio baked sweet potato and beetroot with roasted freekeh and salmoriglio 136

sauerkraut 244–5

seaweed buddha bowl with squash, ginger, cucumber, avocado and seaweed 180

pickled seaweed sauce 251

seeds, mixed black multigrain seed bread 52–3

smashed chickpeas and avocado 147

smørrebrød 156

squash buddha bowl with squash, ginger, cucumber, avocado and seaweed 180–1

camargue red rice with squash and cavolo nero 178

roast fennel, squash, chorizo and basil frittata 118–19

soju korean pickled fruit in soju and honey 258

soup gazpacho 152

mushroom and farro 188

pappa al pomodoro 162

puy lentil and freekeh with chorizo 186

spanish bread and almond 154

sourdough 7, 10, 15, 20

and starter for 22–5

buckwheat, hazelnut and dried apricot sourdough 38

fig, almond and cinnamon sourdough 40

istanbul scrambled egg sourdough with feta and chorizo 142–3

kimchi, egg and avocado on sourdough 144

kimchi sourdough 32

porridge sourdough 34

sourdough blueberry pancakes 44

sourdough french toast with avocado, tomato and labneh 160

spelt sourdough loaf 26–30

Turkish mackerel sourdough sandwich 150

soy pickled eggs 260

spanish bread and almond soup 155

spelt 166

flour 10, 24

savoury spelt pastry 123

spelt and hemp seed granola 196

spelt and poppy seed pitta 60–1

spelt and rye pastry 123

spelt sandwich loaf 54–5

spelt sourdough loaf 26–30

spelt wraps 62

super-fast, no-knead spelt and rye loaf 64

spiced crispbreads 68–9

spiced raisin jam 202

squash buddha bowl with squash, ginger, cucumber, avocado and seaweed 180

camargue red rice with squash and cavolo nero 178

sterilising jars 234

strawberry italian strawberry and chocolate chunk cake 72–3

strawberry, balsamic and thyme jam 204

strawberry, millet, pistachios and goat's cheese 170

sugars 11

sweet potato baked sweet potato and beetroot with roasted freekeh and salmoriglio 136

caramelised onion, sweet potato and rye tart 124–5

overnight sweet potato oats 192

sweet shortcrust pastry 86

sweeteners 11

tahini chocolate, tahini and pecan rye cookies 108–9

coconut, tahini and cranberry macaroons 110

gochujang tahini 219

miso tahini 219

rye with cauliflower, peaches and tahini 176

tahini verde 218

whole baked cauliflower with cumin tahini 130–1

tart apricot 90

caramelised onion, sweet potato and rye 124–5

chocolate hazelnut 96–7

fig and pistachio frangipane 92

hazelnut coconut caramel 88–9

pear 98–9

red onion, girolles and pine nut 128

thyme and tomato 126

teff 167

wild rice, apple, tomato and teff salad 172

thyme roasted carrots with kamut, thyme, hazelnuts and garlic yoghurt 138

strawberry, balsamic and thyme jam 204

thyme and rosemary salmoriglio 215

thyme and tomato tarte Tatin 126

tomato chilli tomato jam 208

pan con tomate 154

pappa al pomodoro soup 162–3

quick red lentil and amaranth dhal with courgette and tomato 184

sourdough french toast with avocado, tomato and labneh 160

thyme and tomato tarte tatin 126

wild rice, apple, tomato and teff salad 172

walnuts pearl barley with smashed cucumber, pomegranate and walnuts 182

wheat 10

wild rice, apple, tomato and teff salad 172

whole baked cauliflower with cumin tahini 130–1

yoghurt roasted carrots with kamut, thyme, hazelnuts and garlic yoghurt 138

three ways (cumin, mint, yoghurt) 228

acknowledgements

Hoards of people go into making cookbooks like these, and I feel incredibly lucky to be a part of the Orion family. A huge thank you to my publisher Amanda Harris, who has been nothing but supportive and a great sounding board from the moment we began working together on *Our Korean Kitchen*. To my friend and brilliant editor Tamsin English, thank you for helping me to shape this book into the beauty it is today; your Irish wit and boundless enthusiasm are unparalleled. To Loulou, Abi and Lucie for your wonderful taste in props and design skills – you completely 'got' what I had envisaged for this book – thank you. Emily, Mark, Sara, Jessica and everyone at Orion – you are the 'dream team'.

Issy Croker – from the moment Jina and I met yourself and Meg we knew you were keepers! You have an impeccable eye, Issy, and I just adore your photos and how beautiful you have made my food look. Thank you.

To my literary agent, Claudia Young – your sound advice and measured approach to everything has been an invaluable asset over the past few years and I am extremely grateful.

To my hard-working assistants, Adam, Katy, Nicola and particularly Fiona Giles – I couldn't have managed the shoot without you.

To Reid Galbraith of Backyard Denim – thank you for the very cool apron, which I am donning on the cover of the book.

To Skye Gyngell, my original mentor – thank you for being so supportive and kind and always finding the time to chat and let me come back into your kitchens for a stroll down memory lane. Thanks also for letting me steal some of your sourdough starter after I smashed my own three-year-old jar of starter on the floor!

To my parents-in-law and all the restaurants and chefs I have worked with in Korea who inspired most of the ferments and pickles in this book – thank you.

To my family, but most especially my brilliant wife Jina – thank you for everything.

jordan bourke

Jordan is a chef and award-winning author. Having trained at the Ballymaloe Cookery School in his native Ireland, he went on to work under Skye Gyngell at the Michelin-starred Petersham Nurseries café in London. He is the winner of the 2013 K-Food Festival, which named him the best Korean chef in the UK, and he was also awarded an honorary ambassadorship by the Korean foreign ministry to promote Korean food in the UK. His book *Our Korean Kitchen* (co-authored with his wife Rejina Pyo) was named cookery book of the year 2016 at the Fortnum & Mason Food & Drink Awards, and also best new cookbook at the Observer Food Monthly Awards. Jordan divides his time between working as a private chef, writer, food stylist and consultant for various food brands and restaurants.

www.JordanBourke.com
Instagram – @jordanbourke
Twitter – @jordanbourk
Facebook – JordanBourkeChef

First published in Great Britain in 2017 by Orion Publishing Group Ltd
Carmelite House
50 Victoria Embankment
London EC4Y 0DZ
An Hachette UK Company

10 9 8 7 6 5 4 3 2 1

A CIP catalogue record for this book is available from the British Library.

ISBN: 978-1-4091-6889-8

Photography: Issy Crocker
Design: Abi Hartshorne
Food styling: Jordan Bourke
Props styling: Loulou Clark

Printed and bound in Italy

www.orionbooks.co.uk

For more delicious recipes, features, videos and exclusives
from Orion's cookery writers, and to sign up for our 'Recipe
of the Week' email visit bybookorbycook.co.uk